MW01257557

# *The World At Large*

# *Book 1: Carpe Diem*

# *by*

# *Adam Mehaffey*

**Credits**
**Edited by J.D Kudrick**
**Cover Design: A.Mehaffey / Angie – Pro_Ebookcovers**
**Photography: A.Mehaffey**

For photography of my travels and more please visit:
worldatlargebooks.com
instagram.com/worldatlargebooks
facebook.com/worldatlargebooks

Book 1: Carpe Diem

2014 Adam Mehaffey

ISBN: 9780986372117

Author's Note: To protect the identities of the individuals mentioned in the stories I relate in this book, I have chosen to change the names. Only the names of public figures and my immediate family members have not been changed. Thanks for your understanding.

# Preface

The following is an account of my journeys throughout the world. What started off as a couple of months to get away for an adventure turned into a ten-year journey of learning, enlightenment, hard times, and moments that will never leave me, including times of joy, sorrow, love, pain, near-death experiences, and experiences nearly worth dying for.

During that time, I travelled to over 60 countries, set foot on every continent, including Antarctica; worked in over half a dozen countries; and saw relics from ancient civilisations and technological marvels of the modern world. I saw the highest peak on earth, the lowest valley, and so much in between. I visited places where they had never seen a white man before and countries ruled by governances ranging from democracies to theocracies to military regimes. I saw the cruelty that humanity can have for each other as well as the love that can bind us all. I fell in love, had my heart broken a few times, and broke a few hearts of my own.

They were the best years of my life as well as some of the hardest. The highs were higher, and the lows were lower. Risks were greater and rewards more fruitful. There aren't many people in life that chose the path I did for so long, but 90 percent of people I meet wish they had, for at least a few months, anyway. And as for the people I meet who have done it, I have never met one who regretted it.

I wrote this book to not only share my story, but to hopefully show people that there is a whole world with endless possibilities out there.... and it's obtainable for most! You don't have to be a millionaire or have the luck of the Irish to travel the world. Desire and an open mind are the only tools you need. Carpe diem.

"I Travel a lot; I hate having my life disrupted by routine" ~ (C. Stinnett)

# Contents

# CHAPTER 1

## THE JOURNEY BEGINS

I had thought about leaving Australia for a while—well, maybe a couple of months. I had always thought for some reason that the grass would be greener on the other side, on what seemed like would be an open page compared to the routine of Australia and its isolation. My best friend from childhood (my dog) had died a few months before, and I felt like I had nothing there for me anymore. So one day I awoke and had two words burning in the back of my mind—the same two words that I had gotten tattooed on my arm one year earlier on my seventeenth birthday: *Carpe Diem*, which is Latin for "seize the day / live life in the moment / take life by the balls." I rang all the travel companies in Australia, bartered for an extra few dollars off here and there, and booked a ticket to London. Just a few weeks later, I was on my way.

     During my flight, a sense of falling and impending

doom swept across me as I awoke to my heart thumping in my chest. A sense of panic quickly consumed me—both my mind and heart beating seemingly uncontrollably, playing their own rhythm independent of my thoughts, out of tune with me but still fulfilling their essential roles.

I had a cloud over my consciousness, causing a sense of confusion. Where was I? What was I doing? What situation was I in? I hadn't been out of my comfort zone for a long time, so why did everything seem so foreign to me? As my collective thoughts started to come together, I suppressed the confusion that my anxious condition had brought upon me, and everything began to sink back into my half-conscious mind. I was a wide-eyed, lonely, and somewhat innocent eighteen-year-old who had come to the conclusion that this was the best thing for me since my life hadn't seemed to be going anywhere—well, except the path of a person who sets out to achieve nothing but yet blames every shit circumstance on anything and everyone but himself and then wonders why everyone else seems to have it so easy.

The reassuring thoughts and reasoning for my situation eventually helped me to start piecing things together in my head. *That's right,* I reminded myself. I was keen to have my eyes opened to the world, away from where I had been raised in Adelaide, South Australia— away from what I had known and grown up with. I was leaving the traps I had fallen into. *Yes, yes. There is a good reason for the situation I am in,* I thought. *This is what I wanted. The reason why I am here is because of my own actions.*

Slowly but surely, a sense of excitement and a childish nervousness filled my spirit, led on by a desire for adventure in places where nobody knew my name ... but then another thought crept into my mind. I was sitting in the middle of a tin can with wings, hurtling along at an incomprehensible speed and an unimaginable altitude over the middle of an ocean where probably no person had ever been on the exact spot I looked upon. And believe it or not, I had actually paid good money for it—and all just to deliver me halfway around the world. Recalling the paranoia I had just left behind, I quietly reminded myself that, yes, sometimes I analyzed too much.

———

I'd selected London as my first destination, and I had a couple of reasons for choosing it. One was because my sister lived there, so I had someone I knew who could help me out and show me around. The other reason was I always figured there would be something fascinating about being in the somewhat center of the world—as I liked to think of the UK, with Europe on your doorstep, Africa somewhat on your doorstep, and the US just across the way. Mainly, I guess it was because anywhere could seem like where the rest of the world had been hiding for so many years after growing up in a seemingly isolated country like Australia, where it takes you five days to drive across it—and if you wanted to, you could probably do it without running into another soul.

I did originally want to go to the US first, but because of the visa I received, England ended up as the best place to go, especially since I didn't have much money and needed to work ASAP.

Thankfully, I wasn't on my own during that plane ride. I was traveling with my sister's friend Lisa, who was a petite but perfectly proportioned, intelligent, deep-thinking kind of a girl—with a fiery streak. She was a beautiful brunette who was on her way to London to live for an undetermined amount of time with her boyfriend Rich, who later would be a part of a night that I will never forget—two people would be involved with a fight for their lives … but that's a story for another chapter.

I still remember when I first landed in London. I can picture myself walking off the plane, through the

7

terminal, and then seeing my sister Rachel. It was the first time we laid eyes on each other in a couple of years, and we greeted one another with the usual less-than-overzealous affection that accompanied most siblings in their teens, but nevertheless, it was good to see her again and to have a familiar face around.

I stayed with Rach in her place, around Paddington in central London. We had seven people in one bedroom, with one kitchen and one living room—basically bodies everywhere when it came to bedtime. But, as people who have done the whole "living in London" thing before know, that's just how it is, especially with Aussies in London: stretch the dollar as far as you can, live off two-minute noodles, and as long as you have money for beer, it's all good—just part of the experience. After I had slept off my jet-lag a day later, it was time to explore. I must have walked around the streets all day just taking in the sights and sounds of London. Every time I blew my nose, it would be black from the pollution, but I didn't care about that—I was just glad to be there. I was on the other side of the world, so it was new and exciting, and it gave me a feeling of really being in Europe—completely different from Australia. It actually physically felt to me that I was on another continent. I stood there and imagined my ancestors living their lives in the UK way back when Australia was not even known to the European world. It even felt a little like where I had come from—and where I belonged. It felt comforting to me, and I truly sensed that, for the first time, I was in a place that would spark my interest at almost every turn.

This, then, was the beginning of a journey that would lead me to almost seventy nations across all seven continents and through hundreds of towns and cities harboring all races and creeds of people—from the oldest to the most modern sights, from the highest to the lowest places, from the hottest to the coldest climates, and it would end up lasting for almost ten years.

———

I had been in London for a few weeks but was still overawed by all the new and exciting—and seemingly endless—history-filled surroundings that provided hours of entertainment at a clip.

Like Nelson's Column—guarded by four massive bronze lions that had been cast from melted-down French cannons after their defeat by the English at the Battle of Trafalgar. Pigeons would flock there by the hundreds hoping for a bit of food, wandering around in the middle of Trafalgar Square with their heads bobbing back and forth and up and down, and so easily and routinely seeming to avoid the trample of human feet—until one would have a bit too much a of a close call and would take off in a hurry, which would startle the others and impel them to take off en masse, but not to any great altitude. Strangely enough, they would only alight to about head height, where they would dodge and avoid people's faces like ace fighter pilots weaving through a dogfight. But it was always enough to startle most of the tourists and have them crouch down with their hands over their face, waiting for the horror to be over.

Or the old charm of Big Ben at the Houses of Parliament. The clock for some reason didn't turn out to be as big as I had pictured it in my mind, but remained impressive nonetheless with the Gothic style it had kept for hundreds of years—like some truly ageless timekeeper watching the people live their lives over the centuries while keeping the pace of life for them as they would come and go.

And the Tower of London, where kings and queens of the past resided in times of turmoil, hiding behind massive stone walls that have passed the test of time for nearly seven hundred years. There, I walked in the places I had heard stories about as a child—tales of where history had happened: the place where Guy Fawkes was imprisoned, where William Wallace's execution began, and where Anne Boleyn was beheaded … just to name a few of the events that took place there over its thousand-year history.

Then there was the Natural History Museum with its endless galleries and massive collections. Truly, if you wanted to see the world but were short on time and money, this is the place I would recommend to you. It has so much to see, mainly because Britain liked to send mementoes back to the homeland during its conquest of the known world while becoming the largest empire by land mass that the world has ever known. Mementoes like the mummified body of the famous Tutankhamun, the boy king of Egypt. Or the Rosetta Stone, a stone tablet that deciphered ancient Egyptian hieroglyphs (of course, it's probably worth pointing out that they actually stole it from the French, who had stolen it from the Egyptians). Or even half of the sculptures from the Parthenon in Athens, which they "collected" from Greece.

————

During the course of my venturing around town over the first few weeks, I had been casually looking for a job (which, of course, absolutely paled in comparison to exploring London, although I didn't have much money). Not surprisingly, I hadn't managed to find anything on the job front, but between Rachel and me, we had managed to find a bigger and better place to move into in an area called Camden. It was on Arlington Road, right around the corner from Mornington Crescent station, and one street back from the main strip—only a five-minute walk down the high street from the famous Camden Market, where on the weekends (particularly on Sundays), it would turn into one of the most famous markets in London. It wound its way around the top end of Camden Street and went down into lane-ways along the canal, under bridges, and then found its way into various levels of the surrounding buildings and even had a big open-air section. It hadn't been built as a market by any means, but with all its nooks and crannies, and its layout diversity, it had plenty of character.

The Camden Market was also known as an "alternative" market, where you could buy anything in the stalls, from trinkets, photography, board games, clothes, and even modern art from the guy who lives around the corner—or the latest nightclub fashions or dominatrix gear. The place came alive with all the colorful characters you can imagine being associated with a place like that.

Our house had four levels, and we even had a view of the Camden Palace—a famous nightclub—from the window of one of the bedrooms.

We were supposed to have eight of us living there, the original seven from the previous house, plus one new guy. Unfortunately, the new guy had a bit of an attitude and looked down on everyone else, with a slight sense of superiority as some authoritarian father figure. Needless to say, this arrangement didn't last long, and after a few weeks of arguments and unpleasantries, he moved out. It's funny how things can get out of hand in those kinds of situations. I never really had a problem with the guy, and we managed to get along fairly well. But as for the rest of the group, just like a pack of wolves, as soon as one of them had a problem with the guy, they all took each other's side and their prey stood no chance.

We did have some great times in that house, though. A guy named Brian and I in particular became pretty close, as we were like two peas in a pod at that stage: both really not interested in work, and our weeks went pretty much the same: Monday as a recovery day and maybe a bit of exploring, Tuesday and Wednesday for job hunting, and Thursday for half a day of job hunting and then we would declare the weekend had begun, so we'd head around the corner to play a few games at a local arcade, then get a bottle of vodka and drink that night and maybe convince some of the others to join us. Then on Friday, we would all get smashed in the house. On Saturday, we might go out for a few cheap pints somewhere, then get lashed at the house. Sunday was our most adventurous day, when we would sleep off the hangover and actually do something a little more purposeful, like explore the markets or London itself. We didn't always stick to this routine, of course. For instance, we heard about a drinking game through a friend of a friend, and then added our own rules to it to play the Monopoly Pub Crawl. Basically, you venture around London and try to have a drink in a pub in every area of the London Monopoly board, which was by no means a small feat, considering the full version of the game had twenty-six properties, therefore twenty-six pints, which would equate to about fourteen liters of beer. But we also played versions in which you either only drank half-pints, or just played stations or even just colors.

It wasn't all fun and games, though, as we did pick up some work here and there to somewhat help pay for all of this in the three months we were there. At one stage, I handed out flyers, then did tele-sales for a bit, and even had probably one of the most annoying sales jobs around. The sales job was set up basically like a pyramid scheme, and we would all gather in an office dressed in suits to hear the bosses spew out bullshit motivational speeches and catchy acronyms like KISS (keep it short and sweet) when referring to sales pitches and such. To their credit, they were somewhat motivational, but to be honest, it was a really shit job and didn't take long for the novelty to wear off. We would receive a duffle bag full of cheap imported crap like SpongeBob SquarePants toothbrushes, plastic water ornament kits, kids coloring books, and literally anything you could think, all made worse by the fact that everything in the duffel bag collectively probably weighed about 20kg.

Our bosses gave us a set minimum price on the items—the lowest we could go to make them money—so it really was all about our wheeling-and-dealing skills. We would walk into shops and give our spiel: "Hi, my name is Adam and I work for a direct import company and was wondering if I could interest you in a few products."

Then the wheeling and dealing would start. For example: start off at £3 for a toothbrush, they say no, make it cheaper at £2, they say no, and finally offer them one for free if they would buy something else that you'd mark up even higher so you would still make a profit on the toothbrush. Overall, the method worked pretty well, mostly because people like the word "free." Still, it was a shitty job, and we worked 100 percent on commission, so we had to work long hours to make any money. Sometimes the income was good: £70-£80 a day, or $250 back then with the exchange rate—about a third of an individual's weekly living expenses for where we stayed. The job just wasn't for me, though, and my enthusiasm waned quickly, especially given the fact that I wouldn't have paid 5p for half of the crap I was selling. Not only that, but I was trying to flog it for many times that over, and that eventually came through in my sales pitches and killed any deals. One day, I felt so unenthusiastic about it, I sat in a park for half the day, chucked a couple of products in the trash, and put a few bucks of my own money in just so I could say I got rid of some stuff but had a slow day. It's definitely time to move on when you start doing something like that, so I quit.

One classic moment from that job that I will never forget, though, was meeting up with Brian after we both worked all day selling products for this company. Brian, you have to know, was one of the most accident-prone people you could ever meet, from almost breaking his neck, almost getting hit by a bus, etc., throughout his life, bless him. When we got together, his face looked pale and he couldn't look me in the eye, so I knew something had happened. He finally told me he had gone into a shop, given his sales pitch, and then pulled out a couple of items to show. In the meantime, he placed his duffel bag in front of the radiant heater, and by "in front," I mean literally touching the heater. It didn't take long for the plastic on the bag to start melting away, then the fabric caught fire and all of the cheap flammable crap inside began to burn. And then it spread and caught on like a wild fire and burned down half of the shop. It was one of those situations that, after you realize no one had been injured and the shop had insurance, you couldn't help but laugh your ass off, and I sure did. As John, the Welsh lad we lived with, said, "You know what, Brian? One day, you will see how lucky you are. You were lucky you didn't burn the whole shop and injure someone. And you were lucky you didn't break your neck and spend your whole life in a wheelchair. A lot of stuff has come your way, but you've been very lucky to escape relatively unscathed." At the time he said this, I felt almost mesmerized, and I still try to adopt this attitude toward life events as much as I can.

———

While living in that house, Lisa and I became pretty close. Many nights, we would stay up drinking and then continue talking for hours after everyone else had gone to bed. We would talk about everything and it always got pretty deep. We just had a connection. Lisa seemed to have a lot of problems and questions that she couldn't see a way past, and when she explained everything to me, I helped her see things more clearly. I would break everything down and rationalize it with her. We felt happy and content sharing each other's company for hours on end, and I will admit that I did develop some feelings for her, and vice versa, but nothing ever materialized from that. It was just one of those connections you make in life, like a castle made of sand—beautiful and elegant with at least the appearance and will

14

to withstand the test of time, but eventually as time passes, the tide slowly creeps in and your sand castle slips back into the sea.

My time at the house also ended up being where I made my first real spur-of-the-moment decision to take a random trip. We had all been up drinking one night, and I'm not sure how it started, but I remember talking to Rich about trips and how fun spontaneity could be. So I decided to go to Paris on the spot—and when I say "go," I mean go! The next morning when I woke up, I packed my stuff and was off. No one believed that I was going to do it, and they didn't believe me when I got back until I showed them my stamped passport. I was so glad I made the trip, because it reminded me where I was in life at that point and that I was again falling into a trap of not really achieving anything.

As for the Paris side trip, I loved my first encounter with the Parisian way of life, and it ended up being the first of about five visits there over the years. By no means was the first trip an easy task, considering France was the first non-English-speaking country I visited—and I didn't know a single word of French, so at times, I found it hard. It was usually difficult to find my own feet in front of me, let alone my way around the madly calming hustle and bustle that is Paris.

A highlight of my time in Paris: I drank wine with some fellow backpackers on the majestic steps of the Sacré-Cœur (Basilica of the Sacred Heart), which is a Catholic church that took forty years to build and turned a hundred years old in 2014. It sits atop Montmartre, the highest peak in Paris, and overlooks the entire city. It is beautifully lit up at night and, in my opinion, offers one of the most romantic settings around. You can sit on the sloping green grass that angles away from the church, with two massive staircases beside it, and you have the lit Sacré-Cœur behind you while able to view the sights of the city in front of you. The brilliantly lit Eiffel Tower stands before you, with its sweeping floodlights illuminating half of the night sky, as though the tower is a lighthouse beckoning the whole world to come and see it. Finally, the old and new Arc de Triomphes show off their well-lit symmetry as if to say "Our triumphs of the past never sleep throughout the darkness of adversity. Watch us as we heed the past and light the way for a glorious future."

While in Paris, I also spent a few days exploring the history and culture that permeated every corner of the city. I even went and paid my respects at Jim Morrison's grave. I also went to the Louvre, but couldn't afford to go in—same with the Notre Dame Cathedral. It was at this stage I realized that, as beautiful as these and other places were from the outside, what was the point of having an Oreo if you couldn't eat the cream filling? So I decided to head back to London, get my shit together, save some money, and come back and do it properly.

# CHAPTER 2

## A NIGHT OF TERROR

After I returned to London and was there for a few days, Rich invited us all to a house party he'd heard about. We all eventually decided to go, except for Brian, who was working that night. It was near Bow Road in east London, a somewhat unforgiving and dangerous place at times, but we were all naïve to this fact at the time. The course of events that night, though, would quickly wake us all up to the harsh realities of life.

We arrived at the party after traveling on the underground, which I personally loved, even though at times it felt like being in a sardine can squeezed between sweaty, stinky people, with no one saying a word to each other and everyone looking at the floor, pretending not to notice the hundreds of people around them, some of them not even an inch away. One positive side of riding the underground at that time, though, was being able to drink while riding, so we got warmed up with a few beers on the way. We finally arrived at the house party to find it already in full swing. I remember having a conversation for most of the night with a couple of people I lived with. I can't recall the exact conversation, but I ended up telling Lisa something that Rich had said to me about their relationship—and that was a mistake.

She ended up getting mad at him, and it started an argument. Soon enough, I wasn't anyone's favorite person that night. The reason I mention this minor event is because of what was about to happen and how it would make that situation seem completely irrelevant. It would show me that there isn't much use in squabbling and arguing over things that aren't a big deal in life (especially when your input wasn't welcomed, or had indeed been told in confidence by another)—because at any moment, life can change, so there's no point focusing on the negative.

Finally, the time had come to leave the party. It was about 2:00 in the morning, and we started walking back to the underground station where we could catch a ride back to the house. So the six of us headed down the road: Rich, Welsh John, Mike, Lisa, my sister Rachel, and me.

We were somewhat scattered on either side of the road, and I could sense an air of tension and a feeling of division amongst us because of the night's earlier events.

I was walking ahead on the right side of the road with Mike when we noticed three guys and two girls coming toward us. The first unusual thing I noticed was one guy crossing the road from our side to the other, striding with what could only be described as a bad attitude and a malicious demeanor. You could just tell by the way he was carrying himself that he was out to cause trouble. He was followed shortly after by a more tentative guy who still had the clenched body language of someone high on adrenaline.

The two of them went up to Rich, John, Lisa, Rachel, and proceeded to briefly exchange a few words. All of a sudden, a fight broke out. Fists started flying in an uncontrolled flurry of panic and adrenaline between the guys. It looked more a brawl than a fight, as clothes were being pulled and wild punches were being thrown as fast as possible to inflict as much damage as possible. The two girls with the group began yelling and shouting for their friends to stop.

Seeing all this and hearing the two girls screaming, I started to cross the road toward the group—a bit tentatively at first, I have to admit—when all of a sudden, I felt a push from behind and then what felt like a punch to the chest from around the side of my right arm. As I stumbled a few steps forward, I turned around to see the

18

third guy of the group just a few paces behind me, wielding a knife in his right hand and coming toward me once again. Sheer adrenaline took over at this stage, and my heart sank at seeing the blade—and only the blade—coming closer and closer toward me. I took a few small steps backward, and then, as he lunged for me with a stabbing motion, I moved to the left side and grabbed for his arm. I saw that he was holding a Swiss Army knife, and as I went for his arm, the blade somehow closed back on his hand. I grabbed at his fist, and now having both the blunt side of the blade and his fist in my hand, I proceeded to squeeze as hard as I could while simultaneously drawing him in closer and twisting his arm at the same time.

When he got close enough to my body, I punched him with my right hand twice in the face. I barely grazed his chin with the first punch but managed to connect fully with the second, then threw him back with all my might. He fell over backward on to the ground, clenching his right hand. I could see that the knife had sliced into his hand, opening a wound that had started bleeding. I didn't know how bad the cut was, but it was enough for him to get up and run the other direction while clasping his hand.

At this stage, I looked over to see John walking away from the other fight, holding his neck, and Rich on the ground on his hands and knees while the two other attackers were leaning over him and repeatedly punching him in his abdomen. I ran over to help him, not really knowing what I was going to do when I got there. As I approached, I kicked one of them in the head, and as the other guy looked up, I reached across Rich and pushed him away.

It wasn't until now that I realized that these two attackers also had knives and that they weren't simply punching Rich, but violently, unmercifully, and relentlessly stabbing him—seventeen times just in the abdomen, to be exact. I started to back off slowly because I knew for sure that if they decided to come for me, I wouldn't be able to do much against them. I looked over and saw Lisa walking backwards, eyes as wide and as innocent as a baby lamb's looking upon the world for the first time, her hands cupped over her mouth as she continued to reel in shock.

The next thing I knew, Rachel was by my side and then she began moving closer to Rich, so she was soon in front of me. That's when the attacker who I had pushed away started coming toward us. Every shred of my instinct was telling me to move backward, but I couldn't leave Rachel standing there between us. But by the time I strode forward to be next to Rachel, he was lunging at her with his knife. I pushed Rachel backward with my shoulder as I put my body in front of hers, then I managed to push his arm down as he came in. Thankfully, the knife missed both of us.

At that moment, one of the girls who had arrived with the attackers intervened and dragged our attacker away. The two girls had never stopped yelling and screaming during the fight, pleading with their friends to leave us alone, but their cries had fallen upon deaf ears— until now.

For some reason—I still have no idea why—he decided to listen. It was almost like the physical contact of her grabbing him snapped him out of his rage and thirst for blood. After that, they all decided to walk away, and I certainly had no intention of trying to stop them.

The next moments of that night are still somewhat of a blur. I remember Rich getting up off of the ground, holding his stomach, bleeding profusely there and also from the slash he'd received to his face. I also recall seeing John standing there, holding his throat and covering a slash wound about eight centimeters long. The cut had missed his main artery by a matter of millimeters.

By then, we had all gathered as a group again. I gave my jacket to John so he could apply pressure to his wound and try to slow the bleeding. We all knew Rich was hurt the worst and needed attention as quickly as possible. Lisa went to try and stop a car to ask someone to call for an ambulance. It's quite unbelievable to think, but it was until the sixth or seventh car that someone actually offered to help by calling an ambulance. (We didn't find out until later, but one of the girls with the attackers had also called for an ambulance.)

We were doing everything for Rich that we could while waiting for the ambulance. At one point, I experienced a seemingly frozen moment in time that I will never forget—when everything went from moving at breakneck speed to a dead standstill. I imagine that it was like standing in the eye of a hurricane, with the world around you so crazy and destructive, fully and somewhat incomprehensibly disordered, but the immediate space around you so calm and still that it was almost like I wasn't one with the reality of the situation, like I was sitting at home in front of the TV watching the drama unfold.

That's what it seems like to me now as I look back on standing there, watching Rich lying on his back. Looking into his eyes and seeing the bewilderment that might be best described as looking somewhat like a newborn baby, so unsure of the world and his surroundings, with such an innocence that came from the overflow of shock and emotion he felt stretched out shaking on the ground—with Rachel behind him, holding his head. Was he thinking his time might have come? He looked so unsure of the immediate future … Thinking that the cold, gripping hands of death could be but a few minutes away. Uncertainty coming in every breath that he drew into his lungs even as his mind was being plagued by seemingly simple questions: Why? Why him? Why now? Why here? Why this way? We could do little more for Rich than to apply pressure to his stab wounds and assure him that everything was going to be alright. We kept talking to him,

21

encouraging him that things weren't that bad—trying to distract him and ourselves from our hellish reality.

Eventually, after what seemed like hours, the ambulance came, and both Rich and John left for the hospital.

The rest of us were taken to the police station to give our statements about what had happened, and then we were released. It wasn't until later that night that I realized how lucky I had actually been. When we finally got home, I took off my shirt to have a shower and looked in the mirror to see if I had a bruise on my chest where I had been punched. I saw no bruise—but I did see a cut, only about one to two centimeters, but I realized that the person who attacked me had in fact been trying to stab me in the chest from behind. Luckily, the blade had hit my rib and did not penetrate any deeper.

John was released from the hospital the next day with twenty-odd stitches to his neck and was on his way to making a quick recovery.

Rich, on the other hand, remained in a critical condition for three days, in and out of surgery. It was touch and go for a while—and a nervous wait for us all. But, after a couple more days, the doctors managed to stabilize him. He stayed in hospital for about three weeks, undergoing numerous surgeries for his wounds, which included punctured bowels and his liver. Thankfully, he made a full recovery.

As for our attackers, they were finally brought to justice about three years later. The attacker whose hand I cut ended up going to the hospital because of his wound—and because the police knew of his injury from our statements, they tracked him down the next day. The guy eventually provided the names of the other two attackers. Those two, meanwhile, had fled the country when they found out the police were looking for them. A police inspector later told me the story of how they captured one of the men a few years later. The police heard that this attacker had returned to the country, so they knocked on his brother's door—and the attacker himself answered. He tried to pretend he was the brother, but then his brother appeared at the door beside him. The police threw the man up against the wall and read him his rights. "Oh shit," he said.

All three ended up serving time behind bars. The longest sentence was seven years for attempted murder.

They say there are some moments in life that define who you are and shape the person you eventually become as you grow into adulthood. This, for me at least, was one of those defining moments. A little naiveté was lost along with a little more of my innocence that night. It woke us up to the realities of this sometimes harsh, unfair, unreasoning and cruel world.

# CHAPTER 3

## DOWN IN THE DUMPS

My time in the house on Arlington Road lasted for three months, because that's how long the lease was for and no one was overly keen to renew it, mostly because of the high rent in such a great area. We just couldn't save enough money to have the freedom to do what we wanted. Also, it turned out that when we had that many young people from so many different walks of life and upbringings, living in the same place tended to create frequent arguments—and the longer it went on, the worse it seemed to get.

Nothing too serious, but we just got on each other's nerves. I'm talking about things like people not doing their share of the housework, or being too loud when others had to work the next day—or situations like the time I got a little bit too enthusiastic with my alcohol consumption.

At the time, I was sharing a room with Mike, and we were alternating between the bed and a mattress on the floor. I was sleeping on the floor at this stage. Mike wasn't home for the night, and I'd had way too much to drink. Then, when it came time for me to sleep, the uncontrollable spin started and I jumped into the bed because it was much more comfortable. I assumed the internationally recognized "I've drunk way too much" fetal position—and hurled my guts up. I was so bad that I couldn't get up and go to the bathroom or even lean over the side of the bed for that matter. Yes, I spent the night in a pool of my own vomit lying on his bed, somewhat consciously (the state when your mind is going but the body is dead with alcohol poisoning). Mike certainly wasn't happy about that one when he finally came home, and understandably so—but it was laughed off in time.

So it was definitely time for a change. Pretty much everyone went their separate ways. My sister moved to Wilsden Green. Mike got a one-bedroom apartment in Tottenham Court Road right next to his workplace, which was wine shop. Rich (by then fully recovered apart from the scarring) and Lisa moved somewhere near Notting Hill. I had no idea where John went to, but Brian and I moved to Paddington, where we stayed in a hotel/hostel. It was really more of a hotel, and we stayed for about six weeks, having a hard time finding work and just generally enjoying our time in London, or causing a ruckus, some might say.

That didn't last very long, though, because the money went pretty quickly—and I was also loading up my credit card. So I moved in with Rach for about four weeks, and that where I would spend my nineteenth birthday. Things definitely hit home at this stage: I really wasn't doing anything different to change my life. Yes, I was living it up, exploring, and fulfilling my sense of fascination for the other side of my known world, but I was spending money I didn't have—wasting day after day of sitting idly by on the job front. Things had to change—plus I had overstayed my welcome with Rach. Although she would never say anything, I knew how frustrated she had to be with me sleeping at the end of her bed on a mattress cramped up on the floor, and living off 30p packets of noodles, feeding myself for £2 a day. I was just in her space all the time without a real sense of direction, so I decided to leave.

I couldn't really afford to stay anywhere, though. I was a few thousand dollars in debt on my credit card at this stage, and the last thing I wanted to do was rack up more. So I took a small bag with me, and, in a state of self-loathing, I left most of my stuff with Rach and went to Hyde Park, where I slept for a few weeks. I found myself an area in the park amongst some trees hidden away from view. The shrubbery was dense around me, and I had an area of a couple of square meters for me to put my things and move around. If anyone was to come, they would only have come from one direction. And I didn't have much to hide. I used a sleeping bag to keep me warm at night, plus some extra clothes. I would stuff an extra jacket in my sleeping bag cover at night and use it as a pillow. I also had a bottle of water and my guitar, which I would use to busk during the day. There were even a few ponds nearby where I would wash myself and my clothes at night time. For food, I kept a good half-dozen packets of two-minute dried noodles that I would eat raw—a meal that I am still fond of to this day.

I enjoyed my stay in Hyde Park—for the first night. It felt like camping almost, but different people would come out at night and it didn't take me long to grown a sense of disdain toward them. I'd see all types, and I always had to have my guard about me. I saw the scammers walking past, going home from the bar with what they had managed to pick up that night. I saw the alcoholics come to life as they regained consciousness from a day of being passed out and start to argue with each other as they proceeded to try and find the means to get their fix again and block out the pain of this world through their addiction. I saw the junkies come to life as they came out for the night to steal just to feed their habit, or maybe earn a few dollars whoring themselves off to fund their next score and get their next fix. I slept lightly and grew increasingly wary of the people there as I would watch them interact with each other. They were like animals, some of them. But what I feared even more was that these people had nothing to lose, and a person like that has nothing to fear. There are very few types of people in this world more dangerous than someone who is mentally unstable and has nothing to fear or loose.

I ended up having so much time on my hands that I didn't really know what to do. I'm guessing this was at least partially the reason why these homeless people tended to develop or continue bad habits such as alcoholism, drugs, etc. But I wasn't going down that path; I was just out of luck and was keen to bounce back. I was actively looking for a job—buying the paper every day and going for interviews. I was staying positive by seizing as much of my moment as I could in that situation. Luckily, it didn't take long before I landed the perfect job for me at the time.

# CHAPTER 4

## *LIVE-IN*

It was to be my first live-in job, and it would be at a pub called Deburgos in West London. The job was an ideal situation for any traveler, actually, and one that I would recommend to anyone thinking about heading over to the UK. Most of the older "traditional" bars in the UK provided accommodations for their staff—whether that's because the place used to have public accommodations as well and it was no longer feasible to operate that side of the business; or the original owners lived in the upstairs floors; or it's simply a house being rented by the publicans nearby. Whatever the case may be, it works out well. For the owner, it is an attraction to get overseas workers to fill these positions and not have to pay them as much. For the traveler, it's a good deal because you have your room provided—and sometimes even a free meal a day and perhaps a pint if you're lucky as well—and a small wage at the end of the week. I remember how happy I felt that I was able to save 50 a week (the actual wage was about 110 a week, but 60 of it went to entertainment on my days off and a few late-night drinking sessions, and maybe 15 for food). No, 50 quid isn't really much in the grand scheme of things, but it was a much better position for me after past events.

I was the only male employed in the front of house at the bar/restaurant, as tends to be the same throughout most of the world in the industry. Women in general tend to be more friendly to customers, more intuitive, which is a necessity in the job, and definitely a lot better to look at. I got along with three of the waitresses really well, and we always had a laugh together and brightened each other's day, but unfortunately the whole place wasn't like that. The folks who owned the place could only be described as a very dysfunctional Irish couple—Tim and Natalie. For example: One morning, I showed up at work and found the doors locked. Natalie had been scheduled to open that day, but she apparently hadn't, which was unusual to say the least. So I went upstairs and knocked on their door. Tim answered and I could tell I had woken him, given his pajama pants and lack of a shirt. I could also tell by his bulging, bloodshot eyes that he hadn't gotten much sleep and was hungover.

"I need someone to open up … and a till," I said.

"Where's that bitch? She didn't come down?" he asked in his thick Irish accent.

"No," I answered, a little shocked by his response.

"Right, wait here," he said.

He then shut the door in my face and returned a few minutes later with the keys to the building and the two tills that were to go downstairs.

"Here," he said. "She'll be down before lunch."

And then he shut the door again on me.

*Fair enough,* I thought. *Must have been a big night.*

It wasn't long before lunch came along and Natalie was still nowhere to be seen. It really didn't make a difference, though, since we weren't busy.

The day passed by, and it was soon time to lock up. That's when I saw Tim again. He still had his bloodshot eyes, and now I noticed a scratch on his face as he wandered into the bar.

"Right, then, shall we have a beer?" he asked.

"Of course," I replied as he pulled us a couple of pints.

This wasn't the first time I had shared a beer with him. In fact, most nights, he would sit at the end of the bar about an hour before close and talk to some of the regulars and me. Then, after closing time, we would chat over a couple of more beers.

We actually got along very well and never had those awkward silences that happen sometimes between a boss and a worker. I guess you could say he took on the role of a mentor to me more than a boss, since this was my first bar job ever. He was quite enthusiastic about it, showing me how to clean the lines of the beer taps, do the ordering, and whatnot. I think this meant a lot to him because he said that he had gone through barmen like you wouldn't believe, one every week or so. Of course, I found that somewhat understandable, as living in the same place with only women could be a bit of a challenge sometimes—plus the long hours. Half the time, it was split-shift work, so I would lose my whole day, it seemed like. The wages were low, and the work at times was physical—restocking the fridges, moving the kegs in the cellar, etc. But I wasn't afraid of hard work and came to enjoy all of it, really. As I was speaking to Tim that night, I didn't want to pry and ask about what was going on, so I just kept the conversation light until he finally brought it up.

"I don't know what it is about women," he said.

"What do you mean?" I replied.

"I just don't understand that one," he said, referring to Natalie.

"I love her—I really do—but the things she does sometimes really frustrate me. And not only that, but she knows how to get me going, wind me up, just keep on pushing me and pushing me until I'm so wound up like a coil, I just burst."

"Well," I said, feeling mighty philosophical (probably thanks to the beer), "unfortunately a lot of relationships are like that. People just don't know when to quit. They take their frustrations out on each other because it's the easiest thing to do. We get frustrated because we're around them so much, especially when you work together as well as live together. We spend so much time in this industry trying to put on a bright and smiley face to customers who can be complete assholes. And that's the last charade we want to keep up when we get behind closed doors, so to speak. So it all flies out, especially if you don't have another way to vent all this."

He nodded. "You're so right. It's so much easier when someone explains it to you from an outside point of view."

We continued talking about love and relationships well into the morning and really bonded that night. We seemed to have the utmost respect for each other—as alcohol tends to generate sometimes—and that would make it a little heartbreaking when I betrayed his trust just a few weeks later. It wasn't until about a week later that Natalie finally showed her face around the place. She said that she had a death in the family and she had to run off without notice—which I thought was a bit odd, considering Tim had never mentioned that. But, because it was a personal matter, I never asked anything else about it. At this point, it was summertime—and a great time to be in London. The beer garden was packed most nights and absolutely heaving on the weekends. Times were good and time flew by for us. We would fill our spare time by drinking the nights away and making up stupid songs on the guitar about how shit a coworker's country was (the three waitresses I hung out with were from Blackpool, UK; Melbourne, Australia; and somewhere in Hungary). Even though Sonya and I were both from Australia, our cities were big rivals, so it wasn't hard to find something to make fun of each other about.

Beyond that, we played drinking games and even dared each other to see who could run farthest around the neighborhood while naked and singing the "Mr. Potato Head Song" we had made up.

The mornings, though, were crap getting up for work again, but we always had a little smile on our face— mostly because we had so much fun, but also because we knew on the split shift, we would only be working from about 10:00 to 2:00, then get to sleep three hours, wake up and eat, then do another five to six hours of work, and then do it all again the next day.

Things were going great, but it was about to all change. One night while drinking out back, we heard a lot of yelling and screaming coming from the upstairs living space. It wasn't unusual to hear the raised voices of Natalie and Tim arguing, but this night it seemed to go on for a while, then stop, then go on. We laughed it off and thought nothing much of it.

But then, as had strangely happened before, Natalie didn't show up for the morning shift. I went through the same routine as before, but this time, Natalie didn't disappear for a week. She came down the next night after the bar was closed and I was the only one in it. I still remember her walking past me, holding her stomach, when I noticed that she had bruises and blood all over her face— and then it finally dawned on me what kind of relationship she and Tim had and what had been going on upstairs all this time.

"Are you okay?" I asked.

She couldn't even respond, though, because she was so winded. Before I knew it, Tim came flying down the stairs, then came up behind her and grabbed her hair. To me, he had the eyes of a possessed man. It almost didn't seem like it was him, and I don't think he even noticed I was there. Something, though, inside of me jigged. "What the fuck!" I shouted. As he looked up, I leaned over the bar and connected my fist with his right cheekbone. He fell backward and she ran upstairs.

"Fuck," I said. "Sorry"—even though I really wasn't. He sat there with his ass on the floor, stunned, as if he had just been snapped back to reality.

"No, no," he said. "You're right. Shouldn't have done that. But it's like we were talking about the other week: you know she just makes me snap."

*Riiiight,* I thought to myself. *Not really.*

I didn't know what to do. I had just punched my boss in the face. *Wait ... Is he still my boss? Do I even have still a job still?* So I did the only thing I could think of and poured a couple of pints, to which he rose up off the floor, sat on the barstool, and proceeded to drink.

"Right," he said. "What's been going on?"

I was happy to change the subject, and we didn't talk about the incident ever again. Just like that, it was over. I didn't get much sleep that night, listening for more noise and wondering what I would do if it all kicked off again. But luckily it didn't. That wasn't the end of it all, though. The next day, I learned that Natalie had decided to tell her brother, another crazy-arse Irishman, and he was not happy about his little sister being whaled on.

I was working in the bar around lunchtime when Natalie came running down the stairs and stopped someone who was charging through the bar toward the steps that led upstairs to where she and Tim lived. Turned out to be her brother, who was on a mission to seek revenge. Thankfully, Natalie managed to stop him by throwing herself in the way and begging him not to hurt Tim—because she loved him, she said. She managed to get her brother outside, where they proceeded to yell and scream at each other ... until Tim came down the stairs. Natalie's brother spotted Tim coming downstairs through the window, and came running inside with a knife, straight at Tim. Her brother stopped in front of him as Tim stood his ground with a steely look of steadfastness and shit-scaredness in his eyes. No doubt, most guys would have run.

I just stood there, thinking about how to calm the situation, when it occurred to me just exactly why this was happening, so I did nothing. I also figured that if he was going to stab Tim, he would have done so already.

"You fucking hit my sister, I'm gonna fucking kill

you!" Natalie's brother shouted.

Tim continued to just stand there. I could see he wanted to run away, but he held his ground with balls of steel. Then Natalie came running back in and eventually defused the situation, and even managed to get her brother to leave. I think he made his point loud and clear to Tim, even though I was more than sure he never had any real intention of stabbing him.

The whole situation started to grind on me and weigh on my mind as I thought about it over the next couple of days. *Why am I caught up in all of this? And how in the hell do I seem to be in the middle of all of this while the rest of the staff is mostly oblivious to the extent and seriousness of it? This isn't my place. and it's not my issue. It's probably been going on for ages—and she never leaves him. He always hits her, then apologizes, and then it happens a few weeks later. Neither of them want to get out of it—so why should I bother? It's like you go out of your way in that situation to risk your job and personal relationships and take sides, which puts you in the bad books with one of them. Then a couple of days later, they have made up but you are still on the wrong side of the one whom you stood up against. You've tried to take a step forward and have the higher moral ground but ended up putting yourself two steps behind.*

As much as I didn't like Natalie, and I really didn't—she was a bossy, annoying bitch 80 percent of the time and nice the other 20 percent—and as much as I could definitely see where Tim's frustrations came from, that was no excuse to do what he did to her. As I started to lose respect for Tim and the whole place over the next couple of weeks, we started taking liberties, like pouring free pints and not paying for food—our way of saying "Fuck you," I guess. But one night, our liberality in helping ourselves to the alcohol went a bit too far.

Sonya and I were the last ones in the place after the

customers had left. Tim had picked up the tills, and it was up to us to finish things off. Sonya went around the restaurant to lock up, so I decided to pour a few jugs of beer and then had her put them outside. After everything was locked up, we went outside, took the jugs, and ran off down the road. I felt a mixture of excitement and nerves. We both felt proud, though, because we had just gotten away with something we shouldn't have done. We stopped down the street, and I remember turning around and looking up at the second floor of the pub—and seeing a figure in the window. My heart dropped, and I said, "Oh shit." Then I told Sonya. I knew it was Tim, and I knew we were in trouble. But we still decided to drink the beer before we went back. We returned to the pub and walked around back to the after-hours entrance. Just then, Tim walked past the door and gave a quick glance in my direction, then paused for half a second before continuing on his way. I wasn't sure if he had seen me, but kind of knew in the back of my mind that he had. The next day, Sonya and I went down to work as usual, and it was a of couple hours before Tim and Natalie awoke and came down stairs.

"What are you doing here?" he asked.

"What do you mean?" I asked.

"I expected you would be gone after I saw what you did last night."

I thought of lying and trying to say that we intended to pay for the beer, but I didn't want the hassle to be honest.

I just tried to apologize instead, but it was no good. He gave us both a couple of hours to pack our stuff and get out.

Yes, I kind of felt that I had betrayed him a little bit, especially since over those eight weeks, he had opened up to me and then I turned around and stole from him and betrayed his trust. But then it dawned on me: *I can't have*

*any respect for someone who does something so low as hit*
*a woman. So fuck him and his bar, too.*

Given the chance, I would do it again … but take
more beer.

# CHAPTER 5

## THE TOWERS

Sonya and I were now unemployed and pretty much homeless, although we both had some money saved.

"Where should we go?" I asked. "What should we do?"

"I'm not sure," she said.

"Ever been to France?"

"No."

I smiled. "Shall we?"

"What? Really?" Those were her exact words as she stared at me with eyes full of curiosity at the certainty in my voice.

I looked straight back at her with a cheeky grin. "Of course."

So straight to the underground we went, where we caught a train to Waterloo Station and headed straight to Dover. We decided to spend a couple of days there before heading over to France. When we arrived in Dover, we managed to find a quaint little pub by the seaside, which had accommodations and a homey feel to it. We settled in for the rest of the day, drank pints, and even participated in quiz night just for a bit of a laugh. Although we had lost our jobs, it felt really nice to be out of that situation—in the kind of way that you can never realize or understand until you put yourself outside of the box.

The next day, we did a little bit of exploring around Dover. We visited the old Roman walls, and later saw the white chalky cliffs that had protected England from invasion for the last thousand years. We then decided to get a meal in town before deciding what else we would do that day. We were walking along in town when I noticed a man in his early fifties or so. This guy seemingly appeared out of nowhere, and I could see him muttering something to everyone he approached on the street, even as he held his right hand to his head and looked really concerned about something. It piqued my curiosity, but he eventually came up to me as well.

"They've gone and done it," he said.

"They went and blew it up. World War III is going to start."

"What are you on about?" I asked.

"The USA is under attack! It's all over the news."

He continued to walk on, so Sonya and I went into the nearest bar to watch the news. Even now, I remember it vividly, seeing the TV footage of the two towers, with one already on fire. *Wow,* I thought. *Surely had to be an accident.*

The crawl on the bottom of the screen read: *"Aeroplane flies into Twin Tower. Uncertain whether accident or terrorist attack."*

*An absolute tragedy ... So many innocent lives lost on that plane ...*

Then, not before too long, a second plane hit the other tower and the gravity of the situation sunk in a little bit more. Something really was going down, I realized. *This can't be a coincidence. One plane, maybe, but two? Unheard of ... isn't it?* This had been planned—premeditated—and someone was out to do a lot of damage and take as many innocent lives as they could on the way. I sat there next to Sonya, in shock along with most everyone else.

Looking back on that moment in time, it was one of most sobering experiences I have ever had. It reminded me that our little way of life—the bubble that society has us living within—is not the actual world. It's just the perceived world that we have built in front of us to assure

38

us that life and everything around us is perfect. But 9-11 made me see that it can all change at a moment's notice—and then what are we left with? After 9-11, I paused to ask myself: "What is important? Who is important to me?" *I don't like the bubble,* I thought. The bubble that burst for me on 9-11 had taken me away from reality and toward the true priorities of life.

As I write this, I can picture everything about that pub as clear as crystal. The bar was a square in the middle of the pub, with rows of four standing round tables down the one side and small little windows with old wooden shutters out the front of the place. The TV hung just above the doorway, and the lady behind the bar had flowing dark brown hair, was slightly pudgy, and looked about mid-forties, with glasses that had a chain connecting the ends so if they fell off they wouldn't go far.

"Bah, who couldn't bloody see that one coming?" an older man's voice rang out from a table across the way in the bar. "They've been bombing the shit out of poor innocent people for years. What do they expect? And now we're going to have to go off and fight for their greed—be their chess pieces in their quest for world domination. Tony Blair [the British prime minister at the time] is so far up Bush's ass, he's probably already sending our guys off to die for them."

He stopped talking and turned his head, slitting his eyes at a darker-skinned fellow sitting at the bar.

"I tell you what, though," the old man continued, "those bloody rag-heads better not try anything here."

I looked over at Sonya and she looked back at me. With that bit of eye contact, we knew each of us was thinking, *Shut up, guy!*

But he continued his rant off and on as we all watched with bated breath for the next development.

"This is no democracy when we are just pawns in another's game," the old man went on. "This isn't freedom.

Screw it. Maybe the rag-heads should just go and take over the United States. Hell, there's already enough Pakis here they're bloody running the neighborhoods around here. That's probably why they haven't attacked London. Yeah, take over the States and I bet there would be less war."

At this point, I chose to break my silence: "Look, mate," I said in a tone that surely sounded slightly annoyed—but as polite as possible. "I know you're just having a bit of a rant, but not everyone here is going to appreciate the way you are stereotyping people and slagging them off."

"What, like that bloody rag-head over there?" the old man said.

The darker-skinned guy turned around and said, "I am British. I was born and raised in Britain."

"No, you're bloody not British!" the old man replied. "You're dark! I bet your parents weren't born here; that makes you not British."

"Give it a rest, mate," I said on behalf of the half-agitated crowd in the bar.

"What would you know?" the old man said. "Where are you from?"

"Australia," I snapped.

Then I redirected my attention to the TV to send the clear message that I didn't want to partake in the conversation anymore. But the old man wouldn't stop.

"Well, you would be the same, and you are probably next," he said. "I'm sure there's lots of those people there as well."

I turned back around. "Now hang on a minute! You can't stereotype people like that."

"Well, it's damn true."

"Trust me, mate, if I was walking around London late at night, I would rather run into a group of religious Muslims than young white folk, speaking from experience."

40

"Whatever," the old man said. "I don't care. America needs to stop leading the world down the drain. That's my point. They are screwing this world up for everyone, and now they are getting what they deserve."

"Now hold on!" I said. "Is everything that America does in its foreign politics perfect? No. Are they holding onto and controlling their foreign interests when democracy fails in an overly aggressive manner? Probably. Is it any worse than what the British were doing a hundred years ago? Far far from it. You slaughtered, conquered, and oppressed much more cruelly than any empire of the past four to five hundred years. Is this democracy that you slag off just a farce? Are the decisions made in our lands of freedom made by people who squabble and argue like petty children? Yes. It is organized chaos, yes, but it has a strong foundation—the thought of freedom of speech and expression, freedom from tyranny and the right for everyone to live their life and express themselves as they choose. Is the path of attaining this an easy and peaceful one? Not always, no. But Americans are the ones who imposed these thoughts and beliefs on the world—and don't kid yourself otherwise.

"I tell you, my friend, the other option is much worse. There is only one thing worse than a hundred people grappling for the power of a country, and that is one man who has all the power, as it would be if you had your way. Trust me, it would lead to oppression, and we have been down that path before. You need to realize, my friend, that both the democratic process we have in place ruling our lives and America as the ruler of the free world are both far from perfect. In fact, in my opinion, capitalist democracy and America are the worst world rulers history has had—except for every other one that has come before them. And you should be glad you live in a place where you can say things like that and not have your head cut off."

When I finished, all I could hear was the TV.

Everyone had tuned into our conversation, and several people looked over at the old man to see what outrageous response he would come out with next. But nothing came; he had apparently been defeated. He had a look of humility on his face that I will never forget.

"Now," I said, "if you wouldn't mind, I want to watch the news."

Our hearts sank as we sat there watching the horrible events unfold. And then people began talking and murmuring as they wondered what all of this meant:

"Could this really be the start of a war?"

"How is all this happening?"

"We live in London. Is London next?"

We sat there for about an hour, contemplating what to do. Sonya wanted to stay with an aunt in London and not go venturing too far, just in case she did have to get home in a hurry. She said it felt like a time when she should be close to family. So, with that thought, the Paris trip came to a halt, and so did my mission to go back there with a bit of money in hand to see and do the things I missed out on before. But I knew I would return one day. After we left the bar, Sonya and I went our separate ways, and I never saw or heard from her again. We had gotten to know each other pretty well over the past few months, constantly living and working together, but then it just ended. We soon became only memories in each other's journey, as it is so often the case for travelers.

# CHAPTER 6

## *"WELCOME TO THE HOTEL DRAYTON COURT"*

I returned to London and ended up going back to the same hostel where I'd previously stayed with Brian. This time around, though, I was fortunate enough to only end up staying there for about five days—which at a hostel means easy time. The solitude of being there by myself didn't take long to weigh heavy on me and let the negative thoughts come pouring in.

I just couldn't believe I was back in the same boat again. Although Tim's bar hadn't been the best place to work, I'd only managed to hold down my job there for just over a month before I got myself fired over stealing from the owners. What was my problem? *Am I that completely useless?* Why was everything going so wrong? If I thought in my mind that for a second Australia would have been a better place to be, then I would have left. But I knew that wasn't an option, as even at this stage I felt Australia would be a step backward for me.

Thankfully, I ended up landing a live-in position working at the Drayton Court bar in West Ealing. Drayton Court's claim to fame was that the famous Vietnamese Communist revolutionary Ho Chi Mihn once worked there as a cook while studying in London.

Even with all my confusion about my life in general, I considered these good times for me. Once again, I didn't have to pay for accommodations. I could eat meals at a fraction of the price, the wage was higher (£125), and I was working amongst other travelers and some locals.

At the same time, though, these were also somewhat

blurry times—excessive drinking and excessive working most every day and night.

For a time, I felt like I had found a home so far away from home. I recall many a night playing drinking games with my partners in crime, the other staff.

One night in the accommodations upstairs, we even had a fire extinguisher fight in the hallway, running around the twisted maze of the various levels, stark naked and having the time of our young lives while not giving a damn—totally running on the adrenaline flowing through our veins because of our fear of getting caught. I still don't know to this day how we got away with some of the things we did in that place, or how I stayed employed there for so long—well, in traveling terms, anyway. It still amuses me.

In fact, I remember the very first day I landed the job and moved in—and how it could have easily been my last day. I hadn't even worked a shift yet and ended up having a few beers with my soon-to-be work colleagues. Games of pool led to darts, and as the night grew older and all the patrons left, the times got even looser—so loose that I remember taking a bet with one of the chefs in the kitchen that I would run up and down the street completely naked for a beer.

Always keen to get naked for a beer, I took on the bet. But when I returned, the chef decided to lock me outside for a bit of a laugh. Fair enough. Right, good joke, but then I started banging on the window for them to let me back in, screaming at not quite the top of my lungs, "Come on! Let me in, you bastards. It's cold out here."

I noticed someone in the window above me and looked up to see the general manager, Mitch, who lived in the upstairs accommodations. Judging by his massive eyes nearly bulging out of his head, along with a deathly glare cast in my direction, he had clearly noticed me standing there buck naked in the street. Mitch pointed his index finger at me, slowly turned his hand over, then with a firm

44

repetitive motion, he curled the pointer toward himself as if to say, "Get you arse here now! You're fucked!" And then he stepped back from the window.

I knew he was coming downstairs, and soon enough, I heard him do just that, with his massive stride pounding down the steps (he weighed around of 130kg and was six-four). He immediately proceeded to usher everyone out of the bar. Then and only then did he let me back in to retrieve my clothes.. To my surprise, his first words to me were not "You're fired" or "Pack your bags," but simply "Get to bed." A good first impression, I know, but with time, he would eventually grow a soft spot for me, and even though he would never show it directly, it would come out in his own authoritarian way.

I considered the Drayton a good place of employment, even though the work was hard and long for the most part. We worked our shifts five days a week and they would consist of either a straight shift (3:00 p.m. until close, including clean-up, so anytime from 11:00 p.m. to 2:00 a.m.) or a split shift (10:00 a.m. to 3:00 p.m., then 6:00 p.m. to close, plus clean-up). Then we had those unfortunate nights when someone would rent space downstairs in the nightclub for a function. On those nights, the bar stayed open until 3:00 a.m., so we would have to work until the event finished. But those usually only happened once every two weeks or so, and as we would rotate shifts, no one had to do it very often.

As with any bar, we had some interesting ... I guess you could call them "characters" who would come in and drink there most days—our regulars. D-GAT Dave was about thirty-five and he only drank double gin and tonics (thus, "D-GAT")—and he had at least seven of them on any given weekday and double that on the weekend. His hands constantly shook, and he had bloodshot red eyes that would progressively glass over with each drink he took. Those eyes, though, could turn into piercing bullets if he had to wait more than two minutes to get his next drink order.

Postman Pat (whose name was actually "John") worked for the postal service (if you hadn't guessed that already), and he only drank London Pride. Pat came in every day after work at about 3:00 p.m. to sink his daily quota of seven pints. He wore massive glasses that came right out of the '70s, almost as big as your face. He had a slender build and a knack for cockney slang. a riddled way of speaking that originated in the east of London among the working class.

For example:

apple and pairs actually means stairs.
adam and eve means believe.
butcher means look.
trouble and strife is wife.
dog and bone is phone and there are many many more.

Basically, it could be a whole coded language that you could use for entire conversations.

Then there was Lonely Graham. He would stand at one end of the bar, drinking his beer and talking to Postman Pat, who would insist on dragging his wife and kids to stand there with him on the weekends. We called him "Lonely Graham" because, no matter what, he would always be in the exact same place drinking, even if he had no one else to drink with, which happened quite often since he regularly came in at off times for the bar, like 1:00 p.m.

One of the strangest characters of all was Bitter Pete, a seventy-year-old man who would claim one end of the bar for himself and never sit down. His name came from his bitter and twisted hatred for the world and everything in it, which meant you when you were serving him. He would only drink the cheapest pint, and it had to be

46

full to the point of overflowing. He once actually kicked up so much of a fuss over a 5p price increase that the bar manager let him continue to pay the old price.

And then there was Mickey, thirty-five and a small guy of about five-four with ginger hair and a receding hairline. Mickey worked in IT—very intelligent and wise as an owl, and really a nice guy. He had traveled the world and had a heart of gold. In fact, many times, we would play darts or pool with him on our days off, and we would even invite him over to the staff accommodations to drink with us after hours. It felt like he was one of us, like no other customer.

The customers, though, weren't the only interesting characters in that place. More than a few of the staff also fit the bill quite nicely. One of them was T—Tanya—who was a manager and always seemed to be in a bad and bossy mood. But as long as you gave her the respect she wanted (but didn't always deserve), you could weed your way past the hard-ass persona and get to her soft spot. She had spiky red-dyed hair and wore a small stud in her nose to go along with a tough East London accent. You could always tell when she wasn't working by the clothes she had on. When she worked, she wore ironed pants and a colored shirt, but otherwise, she would be in some sort of hardcore punk-rock getup that featured denim and a Union Jack.

Another interesting staffer was Mars, one of my favorites—which is why I called her "Auntie Mars," in fact. She was a lovely, sweet girl, and she ended up being the first person to teach me how to cook when I ended up doing a stint in the kitchen for a bit of a change of pace. Well, that and the fact that they were short of staff in there because one guy quit and Adrian the head chef got fired for taking a bottle of cooking brandy one night and getting us all drunk upstairs.

I enjoyed working in the kitchen. It did take a little time to grow on me, but I got into it and it was a great change from the bar. Unfortunately, a lot of the sauces and other items came precooked in a package, and a lot of the food was frozen. But, even though it meant I didn't get to cook everything from scratch, it was okay with me because it was a good way to start learning how to cook. For about 80 percent of the main menu, I just had to know the method of getting the meal ready, not actually cooking it—and that made it easy when I was busy, or when Mars had a day off and I was in charge of the kitchen with another new person. The best thing about working in the kitchen was the specials board. That's where Mars would list the specials of the day, which she cooked from scratch, and that meant she taught me and the other beginner cooks how to actually make them. So, even though we were somewhat thrown into the deep end, it never felt too overwhelming. I eventually learned the basics of soups, what spices and herbs go together with various meats, and, most importantly, how to deep-fry ice cream and a Mars bar. I only got to spend a short time in the kitchen, but it certainly wouldn't end be my last by any means. I also found it comforting to know that I held the same position in the same place as Ho Chi Minh. Who knows, maybe one day I will be a Communist revolutionary leader as well.

Finally, there was one lovely girl whom I became really interested in. I still remember when she first came into the bar with a friend and sat at the end. She was wearing blue jeans and a thick winter coat, which was predominantly red with some light blue patches on the arms, hips, and chest. She had straight, long, dark hair and looked very slim. I thought she had the face of an angel— and the personality to match, I soon discovered. Her name was Kate, and she was from Edmonton, Alberta, in Canada. I didn't realize it at the time, but she and her friend were at the bar interviewing for jobs. I only found out after they had finished their drinks and left, when Mitch came up and told me that he wasn't sure which one to hire. I begged and pleaded for my choice, and lo and behold, after torturing me for a while, he said he was going to hire Kate. This would be a part-time job for her, and really convenient, as she only lived about two blocks away.

Kate had really taken my breath away, and I didn't want to screw anything up with her if I was to have any kind of a chance, so I took my time and got to know her. Soon enough, we became pretty close friends. I would head over to her place after work and we would stay up talking half the night. We would even stay awake to watch her hockey team play—the Edmonton Oilers. The games didn't start until about 2:00-2:30 a.m., and they went for a few hours. Today, hockey is definitely one of my favorite sports, and that's thanks to Kate. She explained all the rules and positions, and even gave me a history of the Oilers and the game of hockey itself. In that respect, she definitely seemed a little like a tomboy. I was having such a great time with her, but as much as I wanted to be with her, I didn't want to do anything to ruin our friendship.

One night, we were totally blasted, and she invited me back to her house. I regularly slept over there a couple of times a week, and we shared the bed—but nothing more. This night, though, she put her arm over me while we lay in bed, and I decided it was time to make a move, so I slowly moved my head toward her and kissed her soft lips for a brief second. At first, I felt no response, so I pressed my lips against hers again, feeling some unease about it because I could tell she wasn't sure about it. I got a little reaction this time, so as I went to kiss her for the third time, I rubbed my lips across hers and gently dragged them down to her chin, slowly sucking her lower lip and then playfully taking it with me a bit before I moved down past her chin and onto her tender neck. There, I slowly sucked a little here and a little there, slightly raising and blushing the skin, giving her goose bumps.

She wrapped her arms and one leg completely

around me, and before long, I was on top of her, kissing her as passionately as I could. Along with turning her on, I was trying to show her that pleasing her sexually meant a lot to me—that I wasn't in it for the "win it in a minute, see you later" like a lot of people are … and like I had been many times before with others. But, alas, for some reason I decided to stop. We were both very drunk, and I guess I didn't want to take advantage of her, even though we were both right there in the moment and quite willing. We never ended up speaking about that night again. The "other night" came up once in a conversation a few days later, but we never discussed it. And we would never kiss like that again.

Our friendship went on like this for weeks and weeks. I wanted more, but she didn't because she was traveling and knew that anything serious would never last, so she saw no point in even trying to start something at all. I also think in the back of her mind that she didn't know whether she could take me seriously because of the reputation I had earned around the place.

I knew that I came across as the "live in the moment, enjoy it now, because you never know what can happen" kind of guy, and she had a more realistic frame of mind. I knew that nothing else would happen between us. It had gone as far as it ever would, so I decided to move on.

Oddly enough, I worked with another Canadian girl at the bar—from Edmonton, too, if you can believe it. Her name was Beth and she had started working there about a month before me. She was absolutely beautiful—five-seven, with dark, flowing hair, a 32c cup size, a tiny waist, and the kind of firm arse you could bounce quarters off of. I knew she had a little thing for me, but she seemed way too shy to act on it. One night, though, a bunch of us were drinking, and eventually we went upstairs to hang out in the room that Beth shared with two other girls. Drink after drink after drink continued to flow until everyone was absolutely plastered and then began to pass out one by one.

50

Beth and I outlasted everyone else, and we went to her bed, which was one of three in the room. I laid her down, slowly took off her clothes item by item, and made love to her—with people snoring in the background. It was exciting and rude at the same time—the thought of other people in the room who could wake up at any minute and bust you. The quieter we would try to be, the more the adrenaline would course through our veins and in turn cause us to make even more lustful sounds. A muffling of the mouth and a bite of the lip were all common place to remind each other we weren't alone.

The next day, I went to work and acted like everything was normal, because it was to me, but Beth started acting a little strange around me. I didn't know why until a couple of days later when she confessed to Auntie Mars that she had actually been a virgin and I was her first, and then Mars told me. I didn't know what to say or how to handle it. I just figured we were all a bunch of promiscuous young people living together. At least once a week, someone would be sleeping with someone else, whether it was someone from work or someone they had brought back to the bar. It was just the lifestyle we lived. But Beth apparently thought it more than that—and resented me for just going on with life as usual. It seemed like she thought that by sleeping with each other, we had started a relationship or something. I did feel a little bit of shame and sorrow for Beth, though. She was a nice girl, but definitely not my type. The way she looked at me, I could tell she wanted to be together, but there was no way that was going to happen. I was the asshole, whether I cared or not, which I did. I was that guy who broke someone's heart for the first time and didn't seem to give a damn. From the outside, it looked like I used her and ditched her. She was so innocent and naïve and I was so wild and free, it couldn't come across any other way, to most.

I didn't know what to do besides let it slide, besides

a brief apology. I guess I wasn't man enough to sit down and talk to her about it at the end of the day, and what made it worse was that Kate found out. The night she learned what had happened with Beth and me, Kate didn't stay for a drink after work, and she left straightaway, which she never usually did. I ran after her and asked what was up.

"Nothing," she said. "Everything is fine."

"Is this about me and Beth?" I asked.

"No, it's not my business."

"Are you sure?"

"Yeah, it's cool," she said.

I stopped on the sidewalk—and she continued walking. So I knew it wasn't okay. She had some strong feelings about what had happened. I just stood there, feeling so frustrated. Kate and I got along so well, and would have been pretty good together—but she didn't want that. Yet, when I decided to be with someone else, that seemed to gut Kate. So frustrating ...

Still, all in all, working and living so closely with people helped us find camaraderie with each other—almost like a family, I guess you could say. I think it was mainly because we all had one thing in common: we were people who had longed for something different and had decided to leave our friends, families, and all that we knew to get outside of our comfort zone for an once-in-a-lifetime experience. And it was an experience that I'm sure none of us ever lived to regret, no matter the trials and tribulations that came our way—and the same was true with 99 percent of other like-minded travelers I'd met through the years.

At this pub, we even had our own theme song that we made up. Well, by "made up," I mean we parodied the lyrics to the famous Eagles' song "Hotel California" and made it into our own for Drayton Court. I will never forget the mischievous nights we spent screaming our own lyrics at the top of our lungs until the early hours of the morning, sometimes even until it was time to go to work again:

On a dark English lane way, freezing rain in my
 hair
Warm smell of London pride, stinking up the night
 air
Up ahead in the distance, I saw a shimmering light
My head grew heavy and my wits grew dim
I had to stop for a pint
There she stood in the doorway
I heard the last orders bell
And I was thinking to myself,
"This could be heaven or this could be hell"
Then she lit up a cigarette and she showed me the
 way
There were naked staff down the corridor
I thought I heard them say …
Welcome to the hotel Drayton Court
Such a lovely place
Now we're all shit-faced
Plenty of room at the hotel Drayton Court
Any time of year, you can buy us a beer

Our minds are drunkenly twisted, we shot all the
 tequila brands
We got a lot of pretty, pretty girls that are more than
 friends
How they dance in the courtyard, naked with sweat
Some drink to remember, we drink until names we
 forget
So I called Mitch the captain
"Please buy me my wine,"
He said, "I haven't given a free drink here since
 nineteen sixty-nine"
And still those voices are calling from far away,
Wake you up in the middle of the night
Just to hear them say …

Last thing I remember, I was
Running naked for the door
I had to find the passage back
To the room I was before
"Relax," said the night man
"there are no morals left to believe.
You can check out anytime you like,
But you can never leave!"

We also had a stretch at Drayton that came to be
known as "Swedish season," primarily because every
couple of months, we would get a couple or three Swedish
students on exchange for work experience. The first group
that came had us shouting, "Thank God! Hallelujah! Praise
Allah! There are three of them!" That was because three of
us guys had gotten pretty tight, and we'd hang out a lot,
playing darts or pool, and we had a bit of a reputation with
the ladies. Adrian was our head chef, from South Africa.
He was as hard as nails and would sometimes tell the story
about when he had been shot for trespassing on a farmer's
land when he was about twenty. And then there was Nezza,
who was a Kiwi, and finally me, from Australia.

Eventually, through hard work and dedication,
Adrian managed to hook up with the Swedish girl named
Emma, who had fiery red hair, but that was about all that
was fiery about her. She was quite pleasant, well mannered,
and, well, basically the complete opposite of Adrian. I
hooked up with Jenny, who was your stereotypical Swede
in terms of looks. And good old Nezza got the plum of the
bunch. Ha. Ella was slightly left of brutal. She stood about
five feet tall, weighed around 80kg, and had massive lips, a
wide face, and a slim nose—and for some reason, she
always made groaning noises every time she turned her
head. Nice person and all, but in terms of our mate Nezza
sleeping with a girl, it was an epic fail. Nezza told us that

he had nicknamed her "the Bucket," for reasons that existed in the bedroom and that shan't be mentioned here.

The second round of Swedish students brought us only two girls: Sandra and her friend Celena—or something along those lines (her actual name was like the opposite of trying to spell out a sneeze, and I could write it down but I guarantee you could never pronounce it properly without the mother tongue). Sandra actually ended up staying and working at Drayton for a few months, even after I had left—not bad considering it was only supposed to be for two weeks—but her friend got fired. I hooked up with Sandra and we slept together a few times. We were both liberal about sex in that respect—fuck buddies, I guess you could say, with no obligations or commitments. One particular night, though, things got a little "experimental," shall we say. Six of us had finished working and were keen for some alcohol, so we took some drinks over to the accommodations and we proceeded to get drunk and play drinking games. By the end, only three of us remained: Nezza, Sandra, and me. That's when I suggested one more drinking game: strip poker. Needless to say, having two native English speakers and one non-native English speaker, who had never even played the game before, it was easy to describe the rules as we wished. It didn't matter what was on the cards; the only hands she won were the token ones we gave her. Sometimes Nezza and I won with three of a kind beating two of a kind; sometimes with two of a kind beating three. But Sandra wasn't an idiot. She knew exactly where I was going with the game, but she seemed more than happy to play along. She lost hand after hand—one piece of clothing at a time, until there was nothing left. Then it turned into a kiss for me, a kiss for Nezza. Then she took my shirt off with her teeth. Then she put her hand down Nezza's pants for fifteen seconds. Then it wasn't long before it turned into the very first threesome for each of us. I have to say, it was different. It felt weird having a mate there and I just tried not to look at him or think about him, except for that split second when we'd give each other a high five. Doing the Eiffel Tower, I believe they call it. Oh, how great it was not to have to wait until the next day to brag to your mate about the cute girl you slept with last night—because your mate was there with you. Teamwork at its finest.

Yes, the Drayton become a place for many new and exciting experiences in my life, including the time when I managed to convince a coworker to do a nude model shoot for me. After that, she became known as "Guitar Girl," as the shoot involved a guitar and no clothing at all. And then there was the time that I managed to convince three other girls to strip half-naked with me for a few "naked and proud" photo shots. Always had to have the photographic evidence … Another day, after hitting a bar and then a hog roast and getting totally drunk, we decided to try out something Nezza was telling us about: "nude up." He said that he and his mates back home would do this when someone had a camera out and was about to take a photo. Someone would shout "Nude up!" and they would all then proceed to get naked and try to get into the photo.

So what do you do when you hear an awesome thing like this for the first time and are completely drunk? Well, you pull out a camera and shout "Nude up," of course. AAAAnd we did—all seven of us … on the top level of a double-decker bus with about six other strangers around us. Granted, it was about 2:00 a.m., but a few people were still coming and going. So we rode the remaining seven stops completely naked, laughing a little and trying to act all casual like nothing was happening when someone walked up the stairs to the top of the bus. When we finally came to our stop, we casually got up, walked down the stairs, and said "Thank you" to the driver, who couldn't believe what he was seeing. We then proceeded to walk the 1.5km back to the bar. To our surprise, when we got there, we found a few coworkers still drinking in the bar after their shift, so we once again casually strode in and sat down to join them.

I did also get somewhat of thrill from the work itself. It wasn't all about getting drunk and seeing how much you could laugh and smile while getting into a little mischief. It just seems that those are the memories that stick with you in the long run. I will always remember a busy evening when the bar was packed front to back, and we had five of us behind the two bars, all getting in each other's way and seemingly getting nowhere. All of a sudden, the boss of the bar told everyone to leave, except for me. He looked at me and said, "You know what to do." We then became like two methodical maniacs, clearing the customers two, three, even four at a time—pouring three pints each at a time while opening bottles of drinks and making spirits with our other hand. It was a good moment and gave me a sense of achievement and usefulness that I thought I'd been missing for a few years.

My time at the Drayton Court would also give me my first real sense of missing something back home. My grandmother and I had always been very close, and she had been sick with cancer for about a year at that point. I had been getting somewhat regular updates from my family about her health, but little did I know that they had not been telling me the severity of her illness. Then, one day, the manager on duty told me that I'd received a phone call from home and I needed to contact them. I knew that something was wrong because they never really called me at work. When I phoned back, they broke the news to me that my grandmother had died the night before. I had always wanted to go visit her if her situation got worse, as I knew there was a chance I would never see her again, but fate and misinformation robbed me of that chance. Apparently it was my Nanna herself who didn't want me to know how sick she was, because she knew I would have flown home to see her right away and once again be stuck in the same endless rut I'd been in before I left Australia. And that summed her up, really: selfless until the end. No matter how much I wanted to go back home, I simply couldn't afford to go to the funeral. I was again struck with the feeling of loneliness—a feeling that I could have done more, made more of an effort, told her I loved her one more time, but it was too late and I could do nothing to change it. Time did eventually pass, and I began to feel better about the situation. As is so often the case in traveling, I might have only known my coworkers and new friends for a couple of months, but we had become the best of friends by the time Nanna passed, so that really helped me through it.

But, as it always does when you are living a life of excess, it all gets to be too much eventually. Nerves get frayed, you stop feeling like you're getting anywhere, and the time comes for you to finally move on. As sad as I was to be leaving, I almost felt a sense of relief, which I would come to realize in full in the following weeks. I knew it was the right move, though. I was banging my head against a wall about a woman I would never be with. Things were changing at the bar as well: good friends were leaving for various reasons and new people were coming and it just didn't feel like the same family anymore. I think that moving on is truly the hardest part about traveling. So many times, you can meet people whom you get along with so well and only have known them for a couple months, but you feel like you have shared memories since childhood. Then the time comes to move on—time to leave behind the memories you have and search for the next adventure, because nothing stays the same and nothing lasts forever.

# CHAPTER 7

## *TO THE HIGHLANDS*

I'd had a fascination with Scotland since I was young, so I always wanted to visit there and first of all learn more about the incredible history of that land—the story of being the underdog against one of the biggest world powers in its day (England) and still holding its own. Plus, the country had managed to hold on to a strong sense of tradition and self-awareness of culture, and I wanted to experience it for myself. Finally, I felt drawn by the scenery of Ireland's rolling hills and massive lakes, and how it seemed like it might have the roots of where I originally came from, as our family name originally hailed from there. So I decided Edinburgh, Scotland's capital, would be my next destination. Edinburgh is an absolutely amazing city, and I ended up staying in a hostel right in the heart of town, only a ten-minute walk from the castle. In fact, I can't really say too much about the rest of Edinburgh because I never really left the center of it, traveling no more than a dozen blocks from the castle in either direction. But I never really felt the need to go any farther, to be honest, so it was okay with me.

Still, I ended up growing a slight attachment to the city, and it gave me a cheeky little smile on my face every time I would think of myself there—one of happiness, satisfaction, and contentment with my surroundings. It would almost become like another Paris to me, and I ended up visiting Edinburgh at least five times during my journeys.

I loved the open grass areas in front of the castle, where you could walk in the summer sunshine with the awe-inspiring sight of the castle towering so close by, perched on its rock right in front of you, Its majestic look straight from a fairy tale was matched by few castles in Europe. It was a place where you could just relax, kick around the football with a few friends, have a picnic, or enjoy whatever outdoor activities you felt so inclined to participate in.

I also loved the traditional pubs, the youngest of which was a couple hundred years old and the oldest ranging back almost seven hundred years. These were places where kings and queens had come for a drink, as well as various famous people throughout history. I also liked how some of these old pubs could only be found by winding my way down side streets and alleys to the point of almost getting lost—and the way even the more modern ones still serve the traditional food of the country, some recipes so old that no one really knows how long the dishes have been around for, like haggis or black pudding. Haggis, if you don't already know, is massive sausage, about the size of your fist, with filling that's made up mostly of the internal organs of an animal (sheep, usually). And black pudding, it's nothing that you would think of when it comes to traditional pudding and what it looks or tastes like. Black pudding is animal blood mixed with oatmeal so that the blood will congeal, and then it's all pan-fried. Oh, and one more: white pudding uses pork meat and fat instead of blood. They may not sound like it, but these dishes are all delicious and definitely meals that should any meat lover should try.

(On a side note, a must for any traveler to Scotland is a yellow card, which is technically a discount card for students, but I didn't have any trouble getting one. The yellow card is essential because it gives you discounts on food and drink across Scotland.)

As for the castle itself, well, Edinburgh's is one of the best I have ever seen—in the top five for sure. The castle sits atop a massive rock formation right in the middle of the city, with sheer vertical slopes leading up to the base on three sides, which must be sixty, seventy, and eighty meters high, respectively. The easterly fourth side is a slow decline down to the flat area of the surrounding town, a perfect place for such a structure, really. The castle has been there in one form or another for a thousand years and has been the center point for many historic episodes in Scottish history. It truly is a fortress and has been the home to royals over the years, but these days it houses museums, some of the crown jewels, and plenty of other interesting stuff.

Another favorite of mine was the quirky heart of Midlothian, which is a heart-shaped mosaic on the footpath about halfway up the Royal Mile. (The Royal Mile is the main street of Old Edinburgh that runs from Holyrood Palace, the traditional residence of the kings and queens of Scotland since the sixteenth century, and the Edinburgh castle.) Basically, if you see someone spitting on the ground, you've found it, as it's a tradition for people to openly spit there for good luck. It's a tradition that goes back some two hundred years, and apparently ex-cons first spit there in disdain, as it marks the spot of the entrance to the old prison, which also happens to be the spot where prisoners would be publicly executed back in the day.

Then there was Mary King's Close, which is a walled-off part of the old city. Well, I say "walled off," but it was not only walled off but also ceilinged off—completely built over and intentionally forgotten about—because of the Black Death, a plague that hit Europe and killed about half of the population in the 1300s. Mary King's Close was just one of the disease-ridden areas of the city that they quarantined—or, more simply put, bricked in—and left the suffering to die where they lay. As such, the years since have led to myths and legends of hauntings by the victims seeking revenge and eventual peace. Also contributing to sightings of ghosts and paranormal activity was bio-gas from a nearby swamp. The gas would every now and then flood into this area and the reflection of light would cause eerie light refractions, which would be mistaken as ghosts. Not only that, but if a person inhaled large amounts of the bio-gas, it could cause hallucinations. But that's enough about that; I will let you take the tour for yourself.

I was staying in a hostel just off the Royal Mile, where I would become friends with a Canadian guy named Isaac. We were both broke and looking for work. Eventually, and without even trying to, we both landed a job at the Torridon Hotel, way up in the highlands of Scotland located in a small seaside village called Loch Torridon, as you may have guessed. The village was located about an hour and half west of Inverness on the northwest coast, and on a clear day, I could see the Isle of Skye—the largest of the Inner Hebrides island chain.

The pay for the position would be about the same as my previous pub jobs: £130 a week, but we would end up getting tips as well, so that could add up to another £30 a week. So, with room and board included, and with being able to bring our own beer into the place and not having to pay for anything else besides cigarettes, I could save about £120 a week, which ended up by far my best pay yet.

The Torridon Hotel was a swank establishment in the middle of nowhere. There was one road in and one road out, with the town of Torridon about 1.5km across the way on the other side of the mouth of the bay, and then another town called Sheildag about 5km along the bank of the loch. The road to Sheildag would wind and twist, and rise and decline more than a few times to make its way there.

The hotel itself was an old estate home that had all the grandeur you would expect of a building built by a rich lord a hundred and fifty years ago. For the most part, it had the appearance of a castle and was lavishly decorated on the inside, with furnishings that you would see on a tour of any palace whose interior dated back to about a century ago: stained and polished hardwood furniture, heavy draped curtains, finely detailed paintings here and there, and lavish wooden panels on the lower parts of the walls. It also featured massive fireplaces that were not just for show, but were designed to quickly and, if need be, excessively heat an entire room. Each and every main room had a fireplace, as did most of the bedrooms. After entering the front doors of the hotel, you walked into a large, open reception area, big enough to be spacious but at the same time not so large as to come across as uncozy. The biggest of all of the hotel's fireplaces sat to your right, and the hearth would be crackling and giving off radiant heat to any weary travelers in the wintertime.

To the immediate left was a Michelin three-star dining room, a formal and, once again, lavishly set place with three massive bay windows for diners to look out of. To the back and left stood a massive staircase, which halfway up turned back around on itself and led to the upstairs rooms.

Directly ahead of you was a hidden entrance to the main office, and to the right was a door and a passage that led to the bar going one way, and to the library and some rooms down the back going the other. To the right after the fireplace and before the hall way was an entrance to another large open area, or drawing room, as it was called. This was where they served afternoon tea with sandwiches, if desired, and at night, guests would come down to socialize, have some canopies, and down a drink before or dinner. It of course had its own fireplace, along with lavish period furniture and large bay windows. To the back and to the left was an entrance to the whisky bar, and through the back corner of the bar was one of the entrances to the library. Accommodations started at £240 per room for a night, which at the time was about US$600. And at the other end of the spectrum was the most expensive room, at about £600 pounds a night, or close to US$1,500. That room had the best of the best. It was a suite. To the rear, you had the master bedroom with a massive four-poster bed, just like you would see in the movies, with the drapes down the sides and more pillows than the world-record attempt for the largest pillow fight. It had a huge bay window with cushioned seating that followed the curve of the window. The view was of the snowcapped Beinn Eighe mountain, towering over the loch, and it had snow on the peak for most of the year. And in front of bay window sat one of those Victorian couches with the four short legs, covered in velvet and open at one end, with an armrest and a round pillow at the other—like the type you might see in the old movies or paintings of girls draped over a couch, getting their portrait done (and I would later get a photo of myself doing the same thing, in the nude of course). There was also a full-sized dining table, living room with couches, a massive TV, some every expensive art, and in the bathroom a Jacuzzi bath big enough for two, along with a shower with multiple nozzles. Although that was the most expensive room, the hotel had a one-up on that, which was known as the boathouse. It was a separate building on the property, completely self-contained (I say "self-contained," but if you were staying in the boathouse and didn't feel like coming to the restaurant, you could have the waiters bring each course of your meal to you there). The boathouse was secluded by forest, right on the water's edge of the loch. It even had its own jetty right amongst the sea birds and otters. And all yours for £1,200 a night or US$3,000.

Right next to the main hotel, in an adjoining building, were the staff accommodations, where we had our own kitchen/dining room and seven bedrooms. We had an atrium out the back, where the kitchen grew its own vegetables. Also on the same property was a lodge owned by the same people, called the Ben Damph Lodge (now called the Ben Damph New Lodge). This lodge was a cheaper place to stay and more for the average joe who came through on a hiking trip. The accommodations were in a square block of brick units with a courtyard in the middle. The interiors were designed to look like log cabins but still had the standard of any four-star hotel. Also there was the Ben Damph bar, which was open to guests, the public, and staff—and where we would get our dinner served to us and spend more than a few nights and days off playing pool and drinking Tennant's Lager, the local Scottish beer. The place even had its own local character named Mick. He was about seventy-five years old (I can't be more accurate than that because even he didn't know his own age), always wore his red tartan kilt, moved at the pace of a snail, was as deaf as a doorknob (probably from all of the hair growing out of his ears), and rode his bike there every day to drink straight whisky for two to three hours around dinnertime. He had the thickest Scottish accent I have ever heard, so thick that not even Scottish people could understand him. Of course, that didn't matter much, because he didn't really like to converse with anyone and was one of the grumpiest people I have ever met in my life, but I think that was the way he wanted it.

The scenery surrounding the whole area was the most breathtaking I had seen on my journey so far, but not breathtaking in the traditional sense like most may think of lavish green grass or colorful flowers springing up everywhere. It was more of the massive, rugged mountains all around with single-lane roads running around their feet. Or the small little creeks and lochs where I had to walk on uneven ground to get to them—where many a day off would be spent swimming and fishing in the summertime. Some of these were massive lochs the size of a hundred swimming pools, where it just felt like very few people had ever gazed on the water before, or swum there, all with pristine blue hazy waters.

On some days off, I'd go mountain climbing and end up on what looked like the highest peak in the area—only to soon discover a little taller mountain a couple hundred meters away, so then I would go climb that one, and so on and so forth. I would regularly come across mountain goats, which somehow managed to move and climb the countryside with the utmost ease.

Of course, it wasn't all wonderful in nature there. I had to face the infamous klegs, insects as big as grasshoppers but that could bite you like a mosquito even through jeans, and also the midges, which were Scotland's version of sand flies, except that they would bite a hundred times harder.

When Isaac and I arrived at the hotel, they had two available positions: one as a waiter and the other as a porter. Because Isaac had waiting experience before and I didn't, I became the porter—and he was pretty upset about that, but I was quite happy. My job entailed greeting guests when they arrived while wearing my tartan kilt, knee-high white socks, shined black shoes, sporran (a little pouch that hangs around the front of the waist for carrying things, like cigarettes, a lighter, whisky, and maybe a wallet, if it would fit), white shirt, tartan tie, and black vest. Truly mutton-dressed as lamb, as some might say. During the day, I would fill my time with various duties that I could somewhat do at my own leisure. I would cut and lay the firewood for the various fireplaces in the lounges and bar areas, and then I would later light the fires for the evening services. I'd also shine and polish all the brass around the hotel, set up the bar for the evening, wait on anyone who wanted a snack or drink, place guests' luggage in their rooms, place thank-you letters in the rooms if they were leaving, park guests cars as they arrived—some of which were Bentleys and Mercedes, even a Rolls-Royce at one stage, although I wasn't allowed to drive the various manual cars that would come there because I did not know how to yet, and it would be another year or two before I would get the chance to teach myself how to do that with a little guidance from a fellow traveler from Lithuania. So, my job was basically the caretaking of the hotel during the day.

At night, I would greet guests as they came down for dinner and serve them canopies: various little finger foods such as duck liver pâté, caviar, escargot (snails), small portions of cooked ox tongue, and various other exotic things served on different forms of tiny, half-a-thumb-sized roasted bread. These would form the first of their seven- or nine-course meal. I'm sure you can imagine that, having never tried these kinds of food before, I would help myself to them regularly.

After the guests had finished dinner, they would come into the whisky bar, where I serve as the barman. We had over 350 different types of Scottish single-malt whisky. I actually found it pretty interesting to work in this bar and learn about all the different kinds of whisky. Being able to detect and define different tastes was quite amazing after time—and trying a couple of different ones every day myself, of course (research for the job, with the owner's guidance and consent) to see how much of a difference I could discover between them. Some had a smoky taste, some peaty, while others were florally scented, or rich and smooth, and so on and so forth. One whisky in particular, though, became a favorite of mine, with the owner's permission (and you'll soon see why I needed permission). It was an Ardbeg thirty-five-year-old single malt from the Islay region on the whisky-making map, and probably the most peaty whisky available. It had a smooth, clean finish and was made from malted barley. This kind of Ardbeg ran at a price of £80 sterling per dram, or about US$220 for 25ml. Wouldn't pay that much myself, but it was definitely worth a try.

My time at the Torridon was awesome, though it

wasn't always peaches and cream. But, truly, looking back now, those months would become some I know I'll remember for the rest of my life, because it's the good times that you remember, not the day where time felt like it wasn't passing, frustrations were high, and you thought it was time to rethink your life. It's really not worth dwelling on the negative things. So move on and make some happy memories—and, for me, one of those memories that I'll always cherish was the night of a wedding at the Torridon …

A few times a year, someone would rent out the entire inn for a wedding. I was lucky enough to be there for one. One reason that we had such a great time was because they wouldn't book anyone into the hotel for the two days and one night before the wedding, so on that first preparation day from about 10:00 a.m. onward, no one was in the hotel. Then the place was ours for almost the next thirty-six hours. It only took us a few hours to set up with everyone pitching in, and it was mainly just to have all the current guests checked out. So by two o'clock, everything was done and it was time to have some fun. It definitely wasn't a seven-star hotel with an abundance of activities, but there were some and we always seemed to make our own entertainment.

The activities manager took us all on the archery range, where we proceeded to shoot at a picture of all the managers on the target board. Then we took canoes out on the loch, and later did some skeet shooting with an 8-gauge shotgun. That was great, as it was the first time I'd ever shot a gun—but definitely not the last, and definitely far from being the deadliest weapon I would wield in my hands. But as awesome as it was to do all this stuff we wouldn't normally get to do during the normal running of the hotel, it definitely wasn't the highlight of that couple of days for me. That would come on the day of the wedding itself.

68

The wedding went off without a hitch. The small ceremony was held outside under an erected white wooden archway that had vines entwined in it. It sat on a perfectly manicured, perfectly leveled, rich green grassy area out front, with a red carpet rolled out between two aisles of about fifteen chairs on each side. So behind the archway stood the castle-like spires of the hotel. To the right were the slowly ascending hills of the Scottish highlands, and to the left was a large open area that was the rest of the property. It rolled on into the beautiful bay of the upper loch Torridon and was quickly cut off by the immediate 700m assent of Beinn Eighe towering into the sky. In the middle of all of stood the groom and his bride-to-be. She wore a beautiful white strapless dress that seemed to flow out from her hips in a frozen sweeping motion and then down the aisle. Not to be outdone, the groom sported a lapelled jacket, bow tie, tartan waistcoat and matching tartan kilt with leather sporran, shiny black shoes, knee-high white socks, and the tag of his tartan garters perfectly placed on the side so as to flow directly underneath his purposefully placed ceremonial dagger.

After the events of the day had finished and most of the guests had made a drunken stumble off to their bedrooms, I was still working in the whisky bar in my full get-up, kilt and all. It was getting late and approaching 1:00 a.m. All the other staff had knocked off and were getting drunk in their accommodations. So there I was, all alone and looking after the one stubborn last guest who had come in with his wife about two hours ago and refused to leave when she did—an hour and fifty-five minutes ago. The guy was an American and said he had the wedding day blues. So he felt like chatting and divulging his words of wisdom about everything he could think of—even though I had never even asked one question, let alone for any advice. This guy was sitting at the counter on his stool, hunched over and leaning in toward me, ever so eager to fill my ears with more of his drivel. Meanwhile, I was leaning on one arm against the back of the bar as if to say "Right-o, I've had enough, mate" with my body language. But somehow, it seemed to be coming across to him as "Oh please, I am so interested! Please do tell me more!"

I can't even remember what he was talking about when, all of a sudden, I saw from the corner of my eye another person peek around the corner, then retreat just as quickly. It caught my attention and I looked over. As I was staring in that direction, a young lady walked around the corner, and without a peep of verbal acknowledgment or a glance of her eye, she casually and slowly walked to the back-corner bay window of the bar (which was only a few meters away from me), holding her strapped shoes in two fingers on one hand, gingerly swinging them back and forth in time with an overexaggerated swiveling of her hips as she placed one foot in front and across of the other. As she reached the bay window, she gave a quick pivot on both feet, then slowly bent over, extending her perfectly shaped ass before she sat down and casually crossed her legs. She reclined back in the seat, and with a flirtatious flick of her hair, she finished making her entrance—an entrance worthy of the gorgeous creature she was.

I couldn't help but put a cheeky smile on my face as I said "Excuse me" to the still-yapping man at the bar, and then I walked over to see if the lady wanted a drink.

"Good evening," I said.

"It certainly is," she replied, seeming to waste no time in being flirtatious.

*Another American,* I thought.

"May I offer you something to drink?"

"I'd love one," she replied. "Can you recommend something?"

"Well, it definitely would have to be a whisky, considering our current location—and, more importantly, the way the bar is stocked."

70

She gave a cheeky little laugh.

"And as to which one," I said, "well, that all depends on the sort of mood you are in."

"Hmm, what mood I am in?" she asked as she tilted her head ever so slightly to the right, as if to say, "Go on, intrigue me."

"Yes, your mood. The different tastes of whisky can complement and even encourage a mood." (I pulled that one out of thin air.) "For instance, there are stronger-tasting whiskies to liven you up, and smooth supple ones to have as a nightcap and put you in the mood for slipping between your sheets," I said while looking her directly in the eye.

She gave another cheeky grin and thought about it for a second, then replied, "Well, how about one that will relax me, get me ready for bed, but not make me too sleepy?"

*Oh snap,* I thought. *Well played.*

"I have just the thing," I said. "I'll be right back."

And on that note, I left straightaway for the bar so as not to linger too long. I poured a Glenfidich fifteen-year port wood-finish whisky and walked right back over, ensuring that I didn't make eye contact with my now second-favorite American in the bar—my self-appointed mentor who wouldn't stop talking when he had my ear.

"Here you are. Try this," I said to the woman. "It's somewhat smooth, and was matured in a port wood cask, so it has a little sweetness to it—a little peaty with a hint of smokiness, as well."

"Hmm, interesting," she said.

The woman lifted the glass, maintaining eye contact with me, then she put her nose to the brim to smell the aroma. Finally, she took a sip, paused and thought for a second, then said, "Hmm, tastes like all the other whiskies."

I nodded. "Doesn't it, though?" I replied in a tone that hopefully placed myself on her side of the connoisseur nonsense thing. "But I wouldn't be doing my job if I didn't at least try."

At that, we both let out a little laugh.

"Excuse me! Can I have another drink?"

I turned. My other American friend was hailing me with a little bit of attitude, seeming to imply that this lady had stolen me away from him.

"Certainly," I said.

The woman gave me a strange look, as if to say, "What's up with him?" And my subsequent slight rolling of my eyes replied in kind: "Yeah, he's just one of those."

I leaned toward her and said, "Why don't you come sit at the bar and keep me company?"

She smiled. "Looks like you could use some help over there. And don't worry, I've got this," she whispered.

She got up and led the way to the bar and sat down at the opposite end of the gentleman.

"You're Mike, right?" she asked the guy.

"Yeah," he slurred. "Do I know you?"

"Ahhh, we were just at the same wedding," she said, then laughed.

"Oh … yeah, right," he said.

I just stood there, enjoying the show.

"Where you from—New York?" she asked.

"Right," he replied.

"I'm from Texas," she said. "You know the groom?"

"Yep," he replied shortly and sharply, as if to make it clear that he wasn't interested in a conversation with her.

"You seem a little drunk there," she said. "You Yanks can't handle your booze." She smiled, but it was still a challenge.

"Ha! Better than you Southerners," he replied.

"We'll have to see about that," she said, then looked at me and winked. "Two shots, please, kind sir."

I smiled because I knew where she was going with

this. "Yes, ma'am," I said.

Soon enough, she lifted her glass and said "Cheers" to the man.

Then they both threw back the shot.

"Two more," she said to me.

With her eyes, she gestured for me to pour his drink first, so that's exactly what I did. As he was watching me, she grabbed the jar of water on the bar, which people used to thin out their whisky, and filled her shot glass with it.

"Here we go again," she said.

She clenched the glass in her fist so he couldn't see the color and then threw it down her throat and waited for him.

This happened four times, and it wasn't until the final round that he noticed her whisky was clear.

"Why are they different colors?" he asked.

She paused, clearly caught a little off guard.

"Special reserve," I said. "It's a rare-ish whisky that the lady enjoys."

"Right," he said with a certain level of bedazzlement—and a sway of his upper body. "I ... I ... ummm ... I am ... off to bed," he said. "Good night."

And with that, he was on his feet and on his way out of the room.

"Ha-ha," I said. "Well done to you ..." I paused as I realized that I didn't know her name.

"Mary," she said. "Mary Calmore from Houston, Texas," she said with an enthusiastic manner as she reached out her hand for me to shake it.

"Adam—Adam Mehaffey," I replied. "From Adelaide, South Australia." And then I reached for her outstretched hand, turned it palm down, and kissed the back of it.

"Oh my," she said. "A true gentleman."

"No, no," I replied. "A real gentleman wouldn't be wearing a skirt right now, would he?"

We both laughed.

"So can I buy you a drink?" she asked.

"Well, I'm not going to say no if you offer, but it's okay. I'm allowed to have a little here and there, so I will just pour myself one.

"Excellent. Whatever you want." She laughed.

I poured myself half a glass of my favorite whisky at the time—a Bowmore ten-year darkest—and took a huge gulp while simultaneously loosening my tie. Then I placed the glass on the counter.

"Wow," she said. "What about the rest of it?"

"The rest of it?"

"Yes. I want to get you drunk."

"Oh really? And why would that be?"

She gave me a coy smile and looked down, playing it up big time. "Because I've never kissed a man in a dress before … and I'm a little shy to ask in case he says no."

"Well, maybe you should just try it and see what happens."

"Well, maybe I will."

She grabbed my tie and pulled me toward her, drawing my face closer to her until she leaned out and pressed her lips against mine. I playfully kissed back, then took my hand and ran my fingertips down the back of her hand, and then ticklishly up her forearm and across her bare shoulder and finally to her neck.

She pulled away. "I'm the only person in my room, so shall we finish our drinks there?" she asked.

"Sure. Just let me pour a couple of the whiskies that will help us stay awake."

The next morning, I sneaked out of Mary's room at about 6:00 a.m. to avoid getting caught by any of the other staff. I returned to my room, got a few hours' sleep, and then got up again. By that time, all the guests had gone, and no one was checking in until the next day. Still, it took a surprisingly long time to get everything back to normal, but

74

at least it was a relaxed time. There were no worries about language around guests or having your uniform primped and proper. It felt nice and casual, and most of us even got to sleep in the next morning as well.

We had everything back to normal by about two o'clock in the afternoon, and that's when the owner had a surprise for us. First of all, he broke out about ten cases of beer, a dozen bottles of wine, and a couple bottles of whisky to share among the couple dozen or so staff members. Second, he divided the £2,500 tip the bridal party had left us, which worked out to be about 100 quid each—an extremely pleasant surprise considering it was somewhat of a whole month's worth of tips for just a couple days' work, which we had enjoyed doing.

And it was on from there—drinking, talking, playing pool, and everyone in awe of my story about Mary from the night before. I even told it to Dan, the owner, who gave me a big smile and said he thought it was a great thing. Of course, I left out the part about where I'd stayed in the hotel and said it had been in the staff accommodation, but who could blame me? So, by about midnight, only five of us were left to party on: Amanda, Frenchy, Don, Jo, Allan (the assistant manager), and myself. We decided to pose for a drunken group photo, when all of a sudden from between my lips slipped the words "Nude up!" Having previously explained my past antics at other places to Allan and Don, it wasn't long before we guys were half-naked, and the girls soon followed suit.

But it got a little boring being naked inside after a while, so we went for a walk outside and started running around the premises like we were in a trance during some kind of Wiccan ritual. But, oh no, it wasn't to end there. For some reason, I thought it would be an awesome idea to get some naked photos in the front of the hotel, so we did. Well, it wasn't long before we were running around inside the hotel taking pictures of ourselves naked—in the entrance room, posing in front of fireplaces, taking pretend spanking photos in the bay windows, and we even charged upstairs to one of the master suites where we posed on the bed. And I got the photo I wanted on that chair, posing just like Kate Winslet in *Titanic*. Somehow we managed to keep that night a secret, and it stayed among us. Thank goodness, too, or we would have all been looking for other jobs, especially Allan, since he was Dan's assistant manager.

The good times had come and soon felt like they had gone. I began to sense that it was time for me to move on again. Sometimes you can stay somewhere too long and taint your memories of the place—and, conversely, sometimes not long enough and you miss out. But my amount of time there seemed perfect, and it felt somewhat easier to leave this time. I think that had to do with a combination of things, like I had done it before, so the thought of leaving wasn't such a shock. Also, this place was a lot more isolated, and as nice as it was for a time, I'd had enough. I also had somewhere to be: a place called Nice in southern France. My father would be competing in a triathlon there, and I was excited to go and watch the race and see both him and my mother again for the first time in a couple years.

# CHAPTER 8

## AN UNPLANNED JOURNEY

I ended up spending about two weeks with my parents. My mother and I watched Dad compete in the famous Ironman Triathlon—a grueling race that consists of a 3.86km (2.4-mile) swim, a 108.25km (112-mile) bike ride, and finally followed by a full-length marathon at 42.3km (26.2 miles). After that, we spent a couple of days relaxing in Nice on the French Riviera and then headed to Monaco. One of the smallest countries in the world, Monaco is home to the super rich and the Formula One Grand Prix race once a year. I still remember taking a tour around the track and just being in awe of how tight it was. It was incredible to think how people could have such reflexes as to navigate around the course at up to 320kmph, with some sections and turns barely twice the width of the car. Not much room for error when you're going at those breakneck speeds.

Strolling down to the harbor was an interesting experience, seeing how "the other half live," as the saying goes: massive 150-foot yachts of the rich and famous—yachts with swimming pools, helipads, and all of the luxuries you would expect. (I probably would have tried to sneak onto one of the yachts if I hadn't been with my parents.)

From there, we toured the Olympic Museum in Geneva, Switzerland, went to the prisoner-of-war camps in Strasbourg, France, and then it was off to England for a final stop. My parents stayed in London for a few days, and I served as their tour guide. But before I knew it, our time had ended and they were headed back to Australia.

I wasn't sure what I was going to do or what adventures, excitement, tribulations, and trials would lay ahead of me on my next path. I wasn't even sure if I was going to work again or just do a bit of traveling.

I had never really thought too much before about the saying "Things in life happen for a reason." I had always been a believer that we are all like rocks rolling down a hill. For some reason, one day we just start rolling faster and faster, and whatever bumps or other rocks we hit on the way don't change anything, because we are all heading in the same direction to the same end. Some of us may break in half and not even make it the whole way. But I later came to believe that we as humans can choose to walk down the hill. We can't always control the obstacles that come across our paths on our way down, but if we have the ability to move to one side, change our path, or even slow down if we gain too much momentum. But sometimes fate puts you in front of a rock so large that you can't go around, so you have to climb over it, and at the top of our climb, we have the chance to stop and reflect. We may even see the most beautiful view—or we may slip and fall. But with a little positive thinking, a lesson can be learned from any rock in life, then it is always a positive and never a negative.

So, with all of that rolling around in my head, I decided that since I was already in London, I would go back and visit a couple of my friends who were still at the Drayton Court in West Ealing. During my few days there, I met an Aussie girl named Louise who was working behind the bar. I remember after her shift one night, we were all sitting around and drinking. Louise grew on me as soon as we met. There was something in her eyes that just made her stand tall above all the rest in my opinion, She was attractive, intelligent, had a good sense of humor, and a laugh that somewhat resembled the cackle of a witch. But it was a laugh so unique that I couldn't help but to fall in love with it.

Although I was offered my old job back there with a

78

pay raise, I decided to turn it down. I had a great time while I visited there, but I moved on—and with a good reason. I'd simply had enough time there, and although I still had positive thoughts about the place, I didn't want to taint the memories and possibly fail in trying to recreate something from the past. I'd had my fill of that place. And I apparently wasn't the only one.

Louise had also had enough of working there, even though she had only been there a month or so. We had known each other for not even a week, and hadn't even shared a kiss, when one night I decided to throw an idea her way. I got down on one knee, got a Burger Ring (a snack chip in the shape of a ring), and "proposed" to her, asking if she would run away with me. She said yes—to the traveling, not marriage. The whole thing was fate, I guess you could say.

So where to go? What to see? What to do? All exciting questions with limitless answers. We couldn't really decide where to go first, but Louise had always wanted to visit one place in Europe: the Greek islands. But we were still in England and had many options of places to visit along our way to Greece. Time wasn't an issue, either. One of the ultimate freedoms I love about traveling is when you have no job and no responsibilities or commitments. You can just go for however long you want until the money runs low. Wake up in the morning and move on, or stay another day. Change your mind at the last second because you heard of a better idea from someone, or roll with the awesome people you met the night before.

So time definitely wasn't an issue, but the money part was. It would have to be more of a beeline trip to the Greek islands rather than a few months of exploration before we ended up there. But we planned to take a land route through Europe for the most part and stop a couple of places to check them out. We finally decided to go to the airport, take the cheapest flight from London to anywhere

79

in Europe, and then travel by whatever other means necessary to arrive at our final destination.

"Okay, Louise," I said, "you watch our bags and I'll go get us some tickets."

"Sure," she replied.

I walked up to the easyJet booking counter and said, "Excuse me, could I have two tickets?"

"To where?" the lady asked me in a slightly condescending tone, as if to imply that I was so stupid that I left that part out.

"I don't know and I don't really care—the cheapest flight to anywhere in Europe, please."

"Seriously?" she replied.

"Yes, please."

She gave me a quirky smile and proceeded to check her computer. "Hmm, there is a flight leaving in about ten hours that will take you to Geneva."

"What country is that again?" I asked.

"Switzerland."

"Oh, nice," I said.

"And when would you like to return?"

"No, that's okay. Just one way is fine, thank you."

She raised her eyebrows at me and gave a little giggle.

*Definitely not words she hears every day,* I thought.

"Okay, well, two one-way tickets it is, then," she said. "The plane leaves in ten hours and it will be £60 for the both (about US$100)."

"Perfect," I replied with a smile.

She proceeded to complete our reservation and I soon had the tickets in hand.

Walking back over to Louise, I felt that the world was an easy place, a simple place, one of freedom and endless opportunities, and it often is if you want it to be. If you want to do something, just do it. On your journey in life, just relax and roll with it—carpe diem—and you will be surprised what great things will be achieved, things that can sometimes seem far out of reach to an unadventurous spirit.

"We're going to Switzerland," I said to Louise.

"Hmm, okay," she said to me. But the look in her eyes said, "Just like that, we're going to Switzerland?"

And my cheeky facial expression hopefully replied, "Yes, it's as simple as that."

So ten hours later, we were on our way to Switzerland. Not long after we'd arrived, the whirlwind thoughts of excitement started to wear off, and reality sank in a little. Neither of us spoke the language, and we needed a place to stay, since we hadn't pre-arranged anything, as we never ended up doing during our trip. It might have been less convenient, but it offered more freedom. We would often stay at the same place as the people we met along the way. If we were tired, we didn't have to venture too far, and if we still had all our enthusiasm and time was on our side, we could make our way to all those less touristy places. So, for us, there was no "We have to get here because we've already booked our stay."

Still, it could be rather daunting trying to speak to a person in a foreign language that you hadn't even attempted to practice before. The best analogy I can come up with it is that it's kind of like that awkward moment in the middle of the night when you wake up and go to the bathroom and accidentally step on your cat's tail. It screams and yells, but you can't understand what it's saying; only by its actions can you presume. So you try to apologize and communicate, but it just doesn't understand. The words coming out of its mouth seem like babble to you, but you still try to communicate the best you can until you either get your point across, try and speak to someone else, go about getting what you need through a different avenue, or eventually give up and go about what you were doing in the first place.

81

It was a shame that we really couldn't stay in too many places along the way. We kind of got the feeling afterward that these were likely places we would never come back to again. But we saw more than most people ever get the opportunity to, and in the end, no amount of time is ever really long enough when you fall in love with a place.

As I mentioned, we didn't really have a planned route, so we hadn't done our research on the places where we stopped, and thus we weren't aware of what there was to see and do. At that time, it wasn't like you could just whip out your phone and jump on the Internet. It was pretty much a case of going to the information center in a town/city and going from there. But one of the biggest problems with the tourist information centers was that they were all aimed at serving tourists with money. They were not really interested in coming up with a list of fresh and quirky free or inexpensive things to try and see for younger people in a new place. And, naturally, the longer you spend in an expensive place, the more money you spend—and for some reason, we tended to hit all of the expensive spots. Now, of course, you can just Google a location, and you can guarantee some broke backpacker has been there before and has an opinion on it.

After Geneva, we hopped on a train to Milan and stayed two nights. While there, we checked out the historical Piazza del Duomo ("Cathedral Square"), which is home to Milan's main cathedral, which was built around four hundred years ago. The cathedral is a massive six-hundred-year-old white-marble Gothic structure with literally hundreds of spires of varying lengths shooting upward vertically from seemingly every available space of the upper architecture. The spires are only matched, and actually surpassed, in quantity by the number of pipes on the massive organ contained within the cathedral, which are in turn only surpassed by the thousands of statues adorning the building's interior. It was definitely a lot to take in, and it kind of felt a bit overcrowded to me, but I guess if it took four hundred years to build the place, a lot of people probably wanted to give their input and make their mark. Well, that's what I gathered from it, anyway.

Much to Louise's delight, this area was also home to ridiculously overpriced designer boutiques. Every brand that Italy is famous for could be found there within its own shop: Armani, Gucci, Versace … everything that the top designers in the world had to offer—not that anything was within our individual budgets, but it was still an interesting place to check out. We walked past one shop and saw a pair of €5,000 shoes in the window or a €4,000 handbag. With all of this purposefully crammed into this area of the city, it felt like sort of a hip, exclusive place to be.

This part of Milan also had all the stereotypes you would see in the movies. Young ladies clad themselves in ultra-expensive clothing and would strut down the street with their butts clenched harder than their hands were on their fifty-year-old husband's wallet. Skin-tight dresses showed off their surgically perfected bodies in a stylish and classy way, with tall designer heels that had hardened bottoms to ensure they make a noise walking down the street so as to draw your attention to them. Plus, we saw massive sun hats the width of the ladies' shoulders, large-framed designer sunglasses, fashionable gloves that definitely weren't for the weather. It was all as common as the little pedigree dogs strutting along on their leashes besides the woman, their little legs moving at a million miles per hour just trying to keep up. It really was an intriguing place for an intrigued observer of perceived classes within society.

After Milan, we were on our way again—back on a train, which was turning out to be expensive. Buying single trips, and at the last minute, was definitely not the way to go, as we quickly learned. Rail passes are the best value and can save you a fortune, up to 50 percent, we discovered. We went to a place called Ancona on the east coast of Italy, and there we caught a ferry to Patras in Greece, where we were hopped a bus to Athens. That whole journey took about thirty hours, and twenty-five of those hours were spent on the ferry. Although this may seem like a lot of time, ferries are probably one of the best ways to get around on long hauls. It is not usually the quickest or the cheapest, but it is relatively secure in terms of your valuables. Plus, you have plenty of room to get up and walk around, and even get some fresh air outside, unlike all the other major forms of transportation. When you take into consideration that you're not paying for accommodations at night, it also makes it worthwhile. Of course, it does mean finding a spot in the corner or getting a row of chairs for sleeping, or even sleeping upright in a seat. But that's what backpacking is all about sometimes. You certainly don't always need a bed to sleep in. Once you fall asleep, it makes no difference if you are sleeping on a ferry, on an airport floor, or in a bed in a Hilton.

From the time we arrived at the bus station in Athens, it was not what I had expected at all. We found rubbish piled up in the streets, homeless people on most corners (and the stench that went along with it), buildings falling apart, and many other structures unfinished and not looking close to completion anytime soon. (This was actually a common site throughout Greece, whether it was commercial property or privately owned, and there were a couple reasons for it. First, there is a tax law in Greece that says if a building is unfinished during its construction, you don't have to pay any property tax, so people start building, and when it gets four-fifths done, they simply stop to avoid the tax. Second, because it is comparatively hard to get a bank loan in Greece, people pay by cash. So they save up some money, get a wall built, save up some more, get another wall built, and so on and so forth.)

There was no way I could have seen a city like this hosting the Olympic Games in just a couple of short years. But they did do it and pulled it off quite well. Maybe I just happened to see the few bad areas, but even so, compared to the standards of the rest of Europe that I had seen, it looked like a dump. But all was not lost for us. Because Greece had its rich history, it also had its own individuality—and it occupied a place in our minds of somewhere far, far away from home that you knew existed because you'd known its name for almost as long as you could remember. In fact, what stood out in my mind probably the most about Athens was the Parthenon at the Acropolis. Besides being able to finally see the rest of the thing (this was the half that the British hadn't pilfered and taken back to London to stick in the museum there, as I already talked about), it truly felt like the oldest—and probably was at the time—thing I had ever laid eyes upon. And when I say this, I don't mean it sarcastically because it was decrepit or anything. I mean it because in all of its weathered and torn state, it still retained its historic beauty. Unfortunately (as I now do regret), we didn't go in. I remember being astounded that they would charge €20 at the entrance. Now that may not seem like much, but it was in fact a whole day's budget. It would become a mystery to me in years to follow to think that I was that close to seeing the inside of the Parthenon but didn't go in. It wasn't entirely my fault, what with the restriction of money, but realistically I had traveled all the way to Greece and I had come within reach of one of the wonders of the ancient world—but €20 stood in my way. Foolish, looking back now, but at the time, it was about the money. Now, though, I figure that having a memory like that for the rest of my life would have been worth much more than €20 in the years to come. And the extra day of traveling we had because of skipping the Parthenon, well, there is no way I can tell you that I was doing anything memorable in that time.

Luckily, this realization did dawn on me quickly, and I wouldn't allow this routine to carry on for much longer. After all, what was the point of starting a race if I was never going to finish it? But, at the same time, I still understand why I did it, because when you don't have much money, it is better to come close than not at all. And we may not have gone in like every other tourist, but we did see a whole host of other things. Other temples, just as old but lesser known and a fraction of the size, were free to see and visit.

We were on our way to go to the Panathenaic Stadium when we just happened to wonder by the tomb of the unknown soldier, which is literally a tomb of an unknown soldier with an eternal flame that relentlessly burns out of respect for all the soldiers that have died in conflicts around the world without a grave. It is really common, and you can actually find a "tomb of the unknown soldier" in many major cities. This site was unique, though, because of the sentries guarding the tomb. The guards (the Evzoni) wear quite literally the most unique and ridiculous uniforms I have ever seen. Never could they be confused with any other soldier in the world. They wear what I would describe as the following:

— a red beret with extending black tassels that look like a horse's tail, except unlike a horse's tail, it's not at the back but just to the side and then extending down over the right shoulder and all the way to the waist line
— a snug-fitting, thick vest that is dark blue and has two lines of about thirty gold buttons running down the breast
— a leather belt as high as the belly button, with what can only be described as two cup holders in the front
— a white skirt with a couple of hundred non-

exaggerated pleats, with the skirt so short that no respecting parent would let his/her teenage daughter wear it on a night out

— skin-tight white, thick stockings, which I presume go all the way up to prevent anything from popping out from underneath that skirt

— blue garters around the knees

— the sleeves on their shirts protruding from underneath the vest are as loose an Abba shirt from the '70s when the arm was extended horizontally, but during their march, the sleeve would only be about a third of a length away from the body

— dark red shoes, but not just any red shoes: they had studs or a metal plate or something on the bottom so you could hear them stomp when they marched along (and when they stomped, they stomped, not only throwing their arms up to an almost vertical position but their legs to a horizontal position before crashing them down)

— and the crème de la crème: a black woolly pom-pom that sat above the toes on those beautiful shoes, with the pom-poms wobbling around as they marched

We stared for what seemed like hours, but of course not laughing too loud; they did have guns, after all.

So eventually we got bored of that and moved on to Panathenaic Stadium. This stadium had been around for about 2,600 years. It had been home to the Panathenaic Games, which were basically like the Olympic Games in Olympia, except only Athenians competed—kind of like the Americans these days have a "World Series" baseball tournament every year but don't invite the rest of the world. The stadium was also the place where they held the first modern Olympics back in 1896. The structure had been built completely of white marble and held about four thousand people. The track was an elliptical length of 200m instead of 400m, giving it a very unusual look. It was an interesting place to visit, and if you get the chance to watch a race there (they still have events there, so it is the oldest stadium still in use in the world), you'll see that it is a strange feeling sitting half a world away from where you grew up but sitting in a stadium in the exact seat where people had been cheering on similar events for the past 2,600 years.

After four days in Athens, it was time to make our way to our somewhat final destination. We were off to Santorini, the southernmost island in the Greek Cyclades. I didn't really know much about the place before this, but Louise had done a little bit of research. Santorini was on her wish list of things to see in Europe. I was always open to new ideas, and it seemed like as good a place as any. We ended up spending about a month there, and it was an awesome place to be. If you've ever seen a typical picture of the Greek islands, where it has all those blue- and white-domed houses on the sides of cliffs that flow down steeply into the ocean … Well, that is Santorini: postcard perfection.

Just before we arrived at Santorini, Louise had been a bit worried that it was getting late in the day. She felt tired and didn't want to go through the hassle of finding a place to stay like we almost always did. But luck was on our side. As soon as the ferry landed, we were swamped by hotel touts. It was after the peak season had just ended and everyone was trying to throw their best price at us to get our business. We ended up going to a nice little place, more like an apartment than a hotel. It had an en suite bathroom, a huge double bed, a couple of wardrobes, a fridge, a desk, and even a balcony. For some reason, that room was cheaper than the twin room, and quite a bargain, being at the end of the season: it was only €15 a night (US$7.50). So we had no problem agreeing on sharing the double bed—to save on money, of course. After all, we hadn't even slept together yet.

I think there were a few reasons why I had been purposefully taking things slowly with Louise. First, I think that it showed respect at the start of a possible relationship—and it showed that I wasn't after one thing, which in turn built a lot of trust. For example, later down the road, she might have said something like, "I'm jealous about leaving you at the bar with all of these beautiful women."

And then I could have said, "Oh, come on, you know I'm not like that. We didn't sleep together for weeks when we first met, remember?"

It definitely had the potential to work a lot better than the, "Well, you might go home with one of them because you did that with me when we met" situation. Also, because we were traveling together, and in a way it was just us against the world, I was a bit more hesitant to take a risk, just in case things got a little bit messy, as being so far away from everyone, I felt responsible for her in a way.

In fact, I didn't even kiss her until we had been in Greece for a few days. I remember the day. We had taken a donkey ride up what had seemed like an impossible hill. It was more like a cliff with a path running up it. You had to clench your legs and arse on the ass, leaning as far forward as you could while the sure-footed donkey was taking the same sturdy strides he had done a thousand times before, throwing you around in the saddle but always managing to keep his balance. The ocean seemed to loom right below us, and the water got farther away as we climbed. The cliff's top edge inched ever closer while we had a view of the sun in the late afternoon, creating a red hue in the sky as the sun went lower into the horizon of the seemingly never-ending dark blue sea, churning the sky a pinky red as it went. It let off the perfect amount of light to bring out the contrast of the bright white-domed houses against the dark brown cliffs.

We eventually made it to the top with our lives and big smiles on our faces. We decided to find a place to watch the sun go down. Walking along the little alleys away from most businesses in a really local residential area, we finally found a little balcony at the top of a staircase that was perched on the edge, overlooking the sea. We sat down, and at that moment, I asked Louise if she had ever heard of Ben Harper. To my astonishment, she said she hadn't.

"Well," I said, "I've got just the song for you."

And as the sun was setting, I pulled out my CD player, gave her one of my earphones, and played "Steal My Kisses." Halfway through, I stole my first kiss.

During our month in Santorini, we even tried to pick up some work, because were keen to stay. Unfortunately, though, it was the end of the season and most of the under-the-table jobs were in the bars. But without tourists, the bar scene wasn't that good, so it was hard to find work. We did have an awesome time, though. We found a little bar that we made our local hangout. It would be filled with at least a dozen people every night, and we became good friends with the manager, so there was always a social feel to the place. In fact, Louise actually did work a couple of shifts there to try it out. Unfortunately, the pay was only about €15 a night, plus tips. Again, though, not being tourist season, Louise made hardly any tips and had to work till the early hours of the morning, meaning she slept all day, couldn't really enjoy where she was, and was still spending money instead of earning it.

Two other things mainly stick out in my mind about Santorini. The first is I remember one day walking through some alleyway where there were stalls set up in front of the local business shops. They were selling all sorts of knickknacks, arts-and-crafty kind of things. Louise and I were looking at a couple of things, and a guy walked up, pulled out his probably US$3,000 massive camera, and proceeded to take a picture—of a postcard! To my amazement, just off to his left, a golden shine was coming from the sun, lighting up the cobble paving on the alley that led from our location to the end of a path that dropped to the ocean. It was an incredible sight that he didn't notice or even take a picture of. It reminded me that we spend so much time and effort trying to find beauty and capture it that we never actually get a chance to enjoy it when we find it. We're too busy chasing after it, and if we do find it, we want to take a photo or video of it so it will last forever, but all we end up doing is looking at it through a lens instead of with our own eyes.

The second thing I remember is the night Louise and I had a drunken argument about something so meaningless that I can't even recall what it was. I felt really frustrated after the argument, so I decided to go for a walk. I ended up in an open field and decided to stop near a boulder and sit down for a few minutes. As I sat down and lit up a cigarette to calm me, I threw my head back—but I was so drunk that I fell backward off of the boulder, flat onto my back while hitting my head. Almost instantly, I sobered up and hardly even noticed the pain in my head because I was so in awe by what I saw in the heavens above me. It seemed like a billion stars blanketed the night sky. I had never seen so many before. I must have lain there for about ten minutes in wonderment, thinking and eventually realizing truly where I was, what I was doing, and how sometimes in life the things that we think that matter really don't. As I was looking up at the same stars that people have been looking at ever since the birth of humanity, it really put things in perspective of how time is fleeting and we need to carpe diem while we still can. You only get one life to live. But if you do it properly, one life is enough.

# CHAPTER 9

# TURKISH NUTS

Soon enough, we arrived in Istanbul after a twenty-odd-hour bus ride from Athens, which included only a five-minute stopover in Thessaloniki. Turkey became the first predominantly Muslim country I would visit, and Istanbul could boast of being one of the oldest inhabited cities in the world—also the only city to straddle two continental plates, the Asian and European.

I definitely did like Istanbul, but being so different from any other place I had been, it took a while to grow on me, and we had more than a few frustrations along the way—the situations in which I would sit back and think to myself: *Damn, this wouldn't happen in the West.* But the differences that brought extra frustration also provided some interesting experiences. For instance, it was quite normal to barter there, something I had not come across before. Also, women tended to be looked down upon more than in a more Western society, and the man was still the head of the family. Plus, it was obvious that the traffic was much more "free flowing," shall we say—but not because of better organization. It was simply because there were fewer traffic rules, so it was every man for himself in his haste—no waiting for lights there. It was also the first (but hopefully not the last) country where I would be a bloody millionaire! But that was because 1 million lira were worth about US$.75 at the time. Their largest note, I recall, was the 20 million note, which put it at about US$15.

There is so much history in Istanbul, and so many events have taken place there that it really does have a life of its own. It's filled with character and begs curiosity. It straddles the mouth of the only sea route between the Black

Sea and the Mediterranean. It was the capital of four
different empires. It has always been one of the largest
cities in the world and one of the oldest continuously
inhabited cities, now at almost three thousand years. It has
stayed true to the mystery and legend that has surrounded it
across the ages. I'm also sure that many amazing things
have happened to visitors in Istanbul throughout its rich
history. For me, too, it was to be the place where one of my
most memorable travel experiences would begin—a lesson
that would help me see the kindness in strangers and the
selflessness that we all have the potential to show toward
others, how much a simple gesture can mean to someone
else and how doing a small little act of kindness can change
someone's opinion forever. But I'll get to that soon enough.

If you find yourself in Istanbul someday and want
an example of the "depth" of the place, go and see the
mosques, in particular the Blue Mosque and Hagia Sophia,
which is actually now a museum. The Blue Mosque
(officially named the Sultan Ahmed Mosque) dates back to
the early 1600s. It is not the oldest mosque in the city, but
it's been there since before my land was even known as
"Australia." The structure was nicknamed the "Blue
Mosque" because of the tens of thousands of blue tiles that
adorn the interior, a fair portion of which have been hand-
painted with various designs of trees, flowers, and abstract
shapes of various designs. The vast, seemingly endless
emptiness of the inside—basically one large, almost
circular open room—strikes you as strange at first. It
appears in stark contrast Europe's Christian churches,
which tend to be elongated rooms with rows of pillars
leading to an altar that is the main focus point, with pews
adorning either side of a central aisle. In the mosque,
though, there is no seating, as all praying is done kneeling
on the floor on prayer mats. When you stand inside, its
appearance is seemingly just as high as it is wide, like
you've stepped into a bubble.

94

The exterior of the Blue Mosque has six massive spires towering toward the sky, with one on each corner and one on each flank. They reminded me of the towers of a fairy-tale castle, with maybe only a couple of windows the whole way up, sheltering some princess at the top as she awaits her knight in shining armor to come along and rescue her. A dome sits in the center at the top, and its blue color gives it the appearance of water flowing down over its perfectly spherical sides. It then flows onward to four smaller domes at four equal intervals around its base, being divided only by the gray of the cement, which gives the appearance of smooth weathered rocks sticking out from this "waterfall," which in turn keeps the flow going, dividing it up evenly between the next four larger domes sitting directly in line with the largest one at the top and perfectly in the middle of each imaginary side created by the square pattern of the four smaller ones, and so on and so forth. The imaginary water, then, flows down toward earth from the heavens, dancing down the waterfall back and forth on the domed rocks, highlighting the perfect symmetry between square and circular, parallelogram and cylindrical, water and rock, yin and yang, God and man, heaven and earth..

In fact, from that one peak of the Blue Mosque, with a little imagination you can see that it is the beginning of symmetry for the whole city from that singular point. From one law, one God, flows the opposite of everything: Christianity and Islam, yes and no, even down to the earth itself: the two continents of Asia and Europe, also visibly seen not too far away.

So symmetrically in tune is the architecture that it even has another mosque just across the other side of the park. The Hagia Sophia stands as the Blue Mosque's symmetrical counterpart.

The Hagia Sophia was a Christian church for a thousand years of its history, swapping back and forth

95

between Christianity and Islam at various stages, all of which can now be seen inside through the layers of different decorations over its history: Muslim depictions that were painted, walled up, or etched over Christian imagery, which had been placed over Muslim imagery, and so on and so forth.

At the hostel where we stayed, we immediately became friends with a couple of fellow travelers, Rob and Gavin. Rob was a laid-back Canadian guy on an adventure to see the world for however long his money lasted. Gavin was another Aussie, in Europe for about three weeks on holiday from his job. They invited us to go out our first night, but since Louise wasn't feeling well, she decided to stay behind. Being a bit lazy and very new to the city, we paid a guy who said he was a taxi driver (you get that often when you travel to places if you're white and foreign: every local all of a sudden is a taxi driver). We asked him to take us to a nice local bar with a bit of music and good entertainment, someplace we could soak up a few beers. Upon our arrival at the driver's choice of bars for us, we couldn't believe how amazingly beautiful, and for the most part foreign, the waitresses were. We went to our table and sat down. Being typical travelers, we had already eaten some thirty-cent pasta beforehand and so just ordered a couple of beers. To our happiness, the brews came with some free beer nuts, an awesome food source when you're backpacking—and being free made it that much better.

It seemed like we had stumbled upon the Holy Grail of bars. We could get cheap beer (compared to what you would normally expect to pay in a bar like this), free nibbles, and most importantly, an unbelievable ratio of good-looking women to men. We were sitting there, admiring the views, and having a chuckle at being so proud of ourselves that we were here. All of the sudden, what apparently was the most popular song in Turkey started to play, and a flow of beautifully dressed women appeared, jumped up on to the stage, and proceeded to dance in a cold, stone-like 1980s Soviet manner: feet planted on the floor, shoulders slightly swinging from side to side with the head following because of a stiff neck, and arms swinging somewhat in time to the music, with each motion ending in a click of the fingers.

We did have a little laugh at them, but were more than willing to let the awkward dancing slide considering their beauty.

When the end of the song came, all the women simultaneously stopped. Half of them remained on stage, and the other half made their way to the floor to mingle. It didn't take very long for the first guy at the bar to work up enough courage to go to the women and start to talk to one. It must have taken him about two minutes before he convinced two of them to go back to his table and join him and his friends.

"The guy knows what he's doing," Gav commented as we toasted our glasses to the gent.

"Ha-ha. Well played, mate," I commented.

I obviously had no intentions myself of doing anything, because of Louise, but I was having a lot of fun looking and catching the occasional glance of one of the beauties. I also could see by the way the guys were drooling that they wished they had just a little bit more courage to be able to go up and talk to them.

"Come on, lads," I said, "they're only women! Don't be intimidated. You just have to stop being so Western and be a little more Russian." I laughed.

They both looked at each other and seemed to know exactly what I was talking about.

"Do you want me to go up there for you and get them over here?" I asked.

I raised my head and looked to the dance floor, making eye contact with one of the women while she was looking in our direction. As I did so, I smiled and her facial expressions went from sour to ecstatic.

Both the lads' eyes quickly swiveled toward me, then shifted back toward each other and then focused on me again. I could tell they wanted me to make a move for them, but they both no doubt thought that it would make them seem like lesser men if they asked me.

"Or maybe I won't have to," I said, as I realized that the girl with whom I'd made eye contact was already on her way to our table—and bringing two friends with her.

The guys looked up, saw them coming, straightened their posture, then put their heads back down, sized up their beers, and took a massive gulp of courage.

"Hello," the lead woman said in a thick, monotone Russian accent. "You would like us to join you now, this is okay, yes?

"Ha-ha, sure," I answered for our group.

We were sitting in a horseshoe-shaped booth, and I was in the middle. Two of the girls sat down next to Rob and the other next to Gavin. All three of the girls had empty glasses in hand.

"Where are you handsome men from? You are not from here, I can tell," the lead lady said.

She said it in a way that implied she thought she was a fantastic detective by deducing this fact, even though we were the only English-speaking white guys in the place.

"I am from Canada and these guys are Aussie," Rob said.

From what I'd seen in my travels thus far, this typically would spark a little bit of interest, but these birds didn't even flinch. It was like they were just going through the formalities and didn't actually care to make conversation.

"And you ladies are Russian, yes?" I said.

"Of course. Where else would so many beautiful women be from?" said the ugliest of the three.

"Riiiiiight," I said. "It's hard to find that much

modesty anywhere else, either, isn't it?"

The guys let out a chuckle.

"So," the third one said. She hadn't muttered a word yet, but now decided to cut off what little conversation we'd started. "You can buy us a drink now!" she said.

"Excuse me?" I said.

"You can buy us a drink now," she said again. "We are sitting with you, and now you should buy us a drink for the conversation."

"Well, to be fair, you came over here looking for a conversation, so maybe you should buy us a drink for the pleasure," I said, smiling.

I was expecting maybe a little smile in return, or some humorous response, but all I got was a stone-cold look.

Then they started a conversation among themselves in Russian.

At that moment, I glimpsed a big, fat, old, bald Turkish guy hopping out of the booth next to us. He pulled up his pants, which seemed to have slipped off of his massive belly. He reached back into the booth, took a tiny petite hand in his, and pulled out a stunning gorgeous girl in her early twenties.

*Bloody hell,* I thought. *Guy must be loaded to have a bird like that with him.*

I continued to watch as he put his arm around her; she in turn put as much of her arm around him as she could, and they walked to the side of the stage. There, she drew back the curtain and they were gone.

*Hang on a minute,* I thought as I made a closer observation of the place. *What's going on here?*

As I looked harder, I noticed that guys were periodically going up to the girls dancing on stage (the ones dancing like a ship's mast sailing in the wind), not joining in, but grabbing their hand and dragging them back to their tables or even straight to and through this mystery curtain beside the stage.

"Ummm," I said, "so what exactly brings you girls here tonight?"

"Working, of course," the lead one snarled. "I thought you were the smart one."

"Do you think we would be seen with all of these ugly people?" the second one said.

I wasn't sure if she was lumping us into her grouping, but I presumed she was. And that's when I started to realize that what I thought at first were slight communication problems because of the language and disinterest on their part, was in fact because they were prostitutes and so bloody high on something.

"Ahhhh, right-o," I said, then immediately stopped talking anymore, still in bewilderment at their bitchy attitudes.

BANG!

The third girl, getting the least attention, slammed her empty glass down on the table.

"Come on, now!" she said. "It is time for you to buy us a drink! What is wrong with you, boys? We are beautiful women giving you our company. You should be buying us our drinks. Your mother would be disgusted with you. She has not raised gentlemen."

We all looked at each other. Yes, it was clear that we had all had enough of these birds.

"And tell me," I said, "tell me what a mother would think of her daughter who opens up her legs for money. Now, if you wouldn't mind, please shut up, stand up, turn around, and go find a big pair of old wrinkly old balls to get smashed against your face for $50, because your rudeness is testing our patience."

The guys' eyes widened as they awaited the reaction of the girls.

The one who slammed her glass down gave me the finger, muttered something in Russian, got up, and moved on to the next table. The second one got up without a care in the world and said, "She can be a bitch sometimes," and then moved on. And as for the leader who had brought the other two over, she stood up, stared at me for a second, eyed me up and down, and then said, "Finally, a real man with balls." Then she walked off.

We looked at each other and proceeded to burst out in laughter.

So we'd had our laugh, replenished the alcohol in our bloodstream, and decided it was time to leave, so we got up and asked for the bill. When the bill came, it didn't take long to realize that it was rather extortionately high. The price of the beers converted roughly into about a dollar each, but wouldn't you know it. Not only that, but they had charged us about $10 each for two bowls of nuts. It didn't actually mention what it was on the bill; it just listed two beers for $2, and an extra $20 charge. So I asked our server to come over and please explain what the extra meant. Maybe it was an asshole tax for being cheeky to the girls, I figured. But, no. He proceeded to tell me that it was indeed for the nuts. I tried to ask him if he could please possibly explain to me how a couple of small bowls of nuts could be so expensive, and not only that, why we were getting charged for something we hadn't even asked for; they'd just brought them along with our beer.

"I'm sorry. It's policy. There is nothing I can do about it," he said.

I wasn't exactly a newcomer to this whole hospitality, customer-relation thing, and knew what an argumentative customer could be like. Although, this time I was on the giving and not the receiving end. And I knew that there was nothing that this guy could do about it himself.

"Can you get the manager for me, please, mate?" I asked.

"Why would you want to speak to him?" the server

asked.

"I want to talk to him about this bill."

I did feel sorry for this guy. I knew he was only doing his job, and I could tell by the look on his face that he thought all of this was outrageous as well.

"I'm ... I'm, uh, not sure, sir," he said. I could see he was afraid to go and get him; he seemed intimidated, even.

"Well, I'm not going to pay for the nuts," I said.

Just as I said that, the manager came over after seeing the fuss.

"What's the problem here?" he said as he looked down his nose at me and spoke in a condescending tone, as if to say, "You are a winging Westerner—not the first, not the last."

*God, why is everyone so blunt and rude around here?* I thought.

"Yeah, I'm not happy with this bill, mate. We ordered the beer at the menu prices. We got the beer. They brought us some nuts we didn't ask for. And now they're trying to charge ten times the price of the beer for the small bowl of nuts. It's ridiculous."

"But every beer comes with nuts," the manager said.

"Well, you can't just decide you want to charge for them," I said. "That's just retarded."

"I don't think so, sir."

My two friends just looked on while we went back and forth.

"Look here, mate, if you're going to try and charge me Western prices, I want a Western level of customer service—and that's the last thing we have been getting tonight. We're not some muppets you can take for a ride here."

The manager shook his head. "You ate the nuts, so you have to pay for them."

102

"We didn't ask for the nuts, so we're not paying for them!" I said.

At this point, we had a nice little crowd gathered: two bouncers, the manager, the server, the three of us, and a couple of curious customers with their prize prostitutes who had come over to see what was happening.

I could see by the look on their faces that they also thought it was joke.

"End of conversation," I said. "You either take the money for the beer, or we stand here all night. Your choice."

He continued to throw his same argument at me for the next five minutes, to which I replied with nothing except for the occasional, "End of conversation."

"Fine!" he finally huffed. "You have made enough of a scene."

"You're the one making the scene, raising your voice to me," I said. "I'm simply standing here saying nothing. I've said everything I need to say."

I looked over and noticed the bright-red face of our waiter, standing behind the manager. I hoped he didn't think any of this was his fault.

"Good, finally reason," I said as I pulled out my wallet and then slammed the couple of dollars for the beers onto the counter beside me.

"Have a good evening," I said, then turned to my friends. "Come on, boys. Let's get out of here."

I only made it a few steps before I stopped at the thought of the poor waiter. I turned around, walked back over, shook his hand, and then reached into my pocket, pulled out the equivalent of $20 (the amount they had tried to extort from us for the nuts), put it in his top pocket and said, "Here, mate, this is a tip for you—no one else. You did a good job."

I turned back around and walked toward the door. On the way, one of the bouncers raised his hand, patted me on the back, and said, "Take care, my brother," and then laughed.

As we continued along our merry way, still gloating to ourselves about our victory, our conversation started to get more intense.

"Wow, I can't believe those guys," Gavin said.

"Tell me about it," Rob said. "Bloody Turkish. They think they are so much smarter and can take anyone for a ride."

"Well," I said, "I don't think it's the Turkish. Eh, yeah! Bloody Turkish! I hate this place. God, I just want to take everyone like that, get them all together, and throw them into the river."

Just as we all shouted in agreement, my foot clipped an uneven part of the pavement. I felt myself drop like a stone to one knee, so I braced myself for what I presumed would be a crunching impact. But it didn't come.

I felt my other leg quickly bow outward as it struggled to take my full weight, being halfway bent. Slowing down as the pressure built up on it, it whipped itself back in only after it seemed like it had gone to almost breaking point.

All of a sudden, my legs were in unison again, and they shot together with the spring of a rubber band. I jumped what felt like about ten feet into the air. I managed to land with all the precision and gracefulness of a cat, spreading my arms and legs like a ninja waiting for the next move from his opponent.

I looked at the other guys with an expression that said, "Yeah, that's how good I am."

"Shit, mate, watch it," Rob said to me. "You'll bloody hurt yourself."

"What the hell are you talking about?" I said in my best calm, smooth ninja voice. "Not many people can make a recovery as ninja like as that."

"Ninja like?" Rob said.

104

"You mean sumo-wrestler like, you goof," Gavin said.

Outrageous bursts of laughter ensued from Rob and Gavin. I just remained in position, pondering what the hell they were talking about. Just then it dawned on me. I was sitting. I wasn't poised like some ninja ready for the next move that gravity had in store for me. I had fallen flat on my ass.

The guys grabbed an arm each and proceeded to pull me up off the ground. They whipped me to my feet, and I could actually feel the overhead streetlights blurring in my vision as I was slung to my feet.

"Shit, did you feel that?" I asked.

"What are you on, crack?" Rob said.

They both laughed at me again.

I responded automatically by placing one hand on each of their chests and pushing them backward. They both fell flat on their arses and had an expression of astonishment as they looked up at me.

"Boys," I said. "I think I just figured out why those bloody nuts were so expensive."

We all bellowed in laughter.

It wasn't long until we came across our next interesting character for the evening.

"Hello, my friends! Hello hello, my friends!" someone shouted to us from behind.

We turned around and squinted our eyes, trying to figure out who this character was, still yelling and running closer toward us.

"It's a bloody Turkish leprechaun!" Rob shouted.

"What the hell?" I said.

"It's a midget hippopotamus!" Gav said. "There's a few around these parts, I hear. Be careful," he added in a David Attenborough *Animal Planet* commentary voice. "They prey on foreign meat, jaws of steel, relentless hunters ... Be ready, lads!"

We all laughed.

"Ha-ha. It's a bloody kid," I said as he came close to us.

He was wearing a suit, and carrying an umbrella and a briefcase. "My friends, I was waiting for you."

"Ha-ha," Rob said. "Oh yeah? How do you figure that one?"

"My friend Peter told you to meet me here," the kid said. "I am Sanjeed, remember? Ooohhhhh, come on now!" His voice whined in a serious manner, from low to high, then back down to a low pitch.

We burst out laughing yet again. We knew this was a ploy by the kid, but we decided to play along to amuse not only him but ourselves.

"Let's go! Hurry, hold my umbrella!" he said.

The next thing I knew, the kid had his briefcase in one hand stretched out in front of him, standing in an astride position. His other hand held the umbrella stretched behind him, which I grabbed onto at the other end.

"Hold on!" he cried.

Rob grabbed my hand and Gav grabbed his, and all of a sudden we were gliding down the street at what seemed like the speed of light.

(Although when I woke up the next day and found bruises and cuts all over myself, I realized that it was more than likely we were running and falling all over the place heading down the street, rather than gliding.)

"We're here! We're here!" Sanjeed said.

He took us into a bar and ordered us sheesha and rounds of sambucas.

"Well, my friends, the delivery man has delivered again," Sanjeed said in his strangely wavy tone. "Now I must leave. But before I do, take this map and take those shots."

"Okay, little leprechaun," Rob said. "Whatever you say."

106

We all went to raise our glasses for cheers when Sanjeed shouted at the top of his lungs: "NOOOOOOO! You must all appease the fire gods." He lowered his chin and stared at each of us in turn. Then, in a deep demonic voice, he said, "Roberto, you must do this to avoid an STD. Gavin-ado, you must do this so you shan't fall into the ways of the Communist. And you, Adam-us, you must do this because you are not drunk enough."

We all stared at each other.

"Sure," I said.

And with that, we lit our sambucas on fire and threw them back one at a time. All went well except for one little hitch. Rob forgot about his beard, and as he threw his shot back, his beard caught fire and half of the hair on his face singed off. He barely even noticed, though, in his state.

And that's the last thing I remember of that night, as the bar soon started to whirl around me.

I awoke in the morning back in bed by myself. Louise was already up and exploring. Apparently, she had been up before I even got home—which was probably a good thing, considering I was covered in cuts and bruises and in cream cheese, which I had apparently bought to eat but had rolled into it during the night. I also had a blue tongue and a circle drawn around my mouth in marker, with an arrow pointing to it, which said, "Sambuca goes here please barman."

*Damn Turkish nuts,* I thought.

# CHAPTER 10

## THROUGH THE KINDNESS OF A STRANGER

One experience in Turkey really stood out in my mind, which I alluded to in the last chapter. Actually, this experience could have taken place anywhere in the world, but it just so happened to be in Istanbul. It was during our last few days there that we decided to go out and have some dinner with Rob and Gavin. We all agreed that it would be nice to find a little traditional restaurant, so after hunting around for a while, we found one hiding down a back alley, near the Grand Bazaar.

The Grand Bazaar was yet another mesmerizing sight of Istanbul. It is one of the largest indoor markets in the world, containing over three thousand shops and entertaining thee hundred thousand visitors a day. It's the place in Turkey where people have come to sell, barter, and trade goods for over five hundred years. In fact, I met a man there who told me that his family had been trading there since it began five hundred years ago. It really piqued my curiosity because, unlike Western culture in the past few hundred years, people in Turkey tended to live in the same house generation after generation, and own the same business from father to son for many generations. I proceeded to ask this man more questions. He told me how Istanbul had seen much in the way of famine, disease, war, and different ruling empires over the years, But soon enough, I saw the sales-pitch look on his face. He ushered me toward his shop to try and flog off whatever he could on me. To get his hands on my money, he'd played on my gullibility and my interest in a good story and that was it.

But who was I to judge. After all. isn't that what life was in this part of the world, trying to make a few dollars here and there to support your family? I decided I needed to look at it in another light. Rather than thinking I was conned and forced into buying something. I realized that I got a souvenir and a free experience. So I ended up buying a small nazar amulet off of him—a round, blue, glass trinket that is supposed to bring good luck; the Western version would be a horseshoe or a rabbit's foot. And as the fable of the amulet had promised, luck would indeed soon be coming my way.

The restaurant we finally ended up in certainly fit the part of a traditional Turkish eatery. The interior was decorated in traditional mosaics and draped with traditional Turkish cloth. The eating areas were like stalls tucked away along the halls that you'd walk through. It almost felt like a karaoke bar that had private rooms. Inside each of the dining rooms was a centrally located table, not too high off of the floor. Pillows and cushions lay strewn throughout the room, inviting you to place them in whatever position you desired to make yourself more comfortable among all of the dark reddish colors of the decorations.

I ended up ordering the most traditional food recommended to me: baba ghanoush, which is a dip made of mashed eggplant and mixed with virgin olive oil and various seasonings. You scoop up the dip with bazlama. Bazlama is a single-layered, flat, circular bread with a creamy yellow color, and it kind of has the texture and taste of an English muffin. For my main dish, I had—what else?—a kebab. That definitely wasn't new for me, as I'd had many drunken late-night kebabs at 4:00 a.m., but I just had to try them when I was in their country of origin. If not, it would be like going to Rome and not seeing the Colosseum.

After dinner, we ordered a sheesha pipe, a traditional pipe for smoking sheesha or flavored tobacco. It stood about three feet tall and was placed in the middle of our table. At the bottom of the pipe unit was a large glass bulb that resembled a vase, and it bottlenecked up into a joint, where the top half was made of metal. At this point, two openings were on either side, where pipes were attached for the drawing of the smoke. Then the unit continued up to the top, where the tobacco was placed in the center in a cone covered with foil, then a hot coal was placed on top. Under the cone was a long pipe that ran all the way down to the bottom, where the glass bulb was filled with water. As you sucked on the pipe, it created a vacuum that would in turn draw the smoke down the pipe, cool, and filter it through the water (which caused it to bubble), then feed it through the pipes and into your mouth. I believe we had apple flavor that night, sharing it among us as we sipped on beers and let our food digest for the next couple of hours, savoring the moment and experience.

During the conversation, we eventually got to talking about how Gavin was going to a place called Gallipoli farther down the coast.

Gallipoli has become like a Mecca for young Australians and New Zealanders, and they go there by the thousands, halfway around the world every year to pay their respects for the lives lost on both sides during the slaughter of the Gallipoli Campaign during World War I.

I myself had always wanted to go to Gallipoli and, as I said, had made my way to Istanbul overland from Greece. Unfortunately, at that point, I had been on the road for about five months without working and my money had all but ran out. I had just enough for a ticket to go back to London to start working again (where, exactly, I was unsure about). It made me a little upset to think I was so close but wouldn't be able to make it, having no idea when I would be able to go back.

Gallipoli itself is about six hours by bus along the coast of Turkey, southwest of Istanbul. During World War

110

I, over a period of nine months, a total of 8,709 Australian soldiers were killed, with 2,298 dying in the first month alone. It was a big screw-up, with the ANZAC (Australian-New Zealand Army Corps) troops being dropped too far north on the wrong beach in an area full of cliffs and ridges—just a logistical nightmare, really. With the troops advancing a few hundred meters within the first evening and not much farther for the whole campaign, the men saw a lot of bloody hand-to-hand combat. At times, the opposing sides called for an armistice just so the mounds of rotting bodies on both sides could be cleared to prevent the spreading of disease as much as possible. Many stories of heroism came from that campaign, such as the story of John Simpson, also known as "the man with the donkey." Although he only spent twenty-four days in the campaign before he was mortally wounded, Simpson was credited with saving the lives of hundreds of men by making his way up and down the gullies with his donkey, and then bringing wounded men back to the camps for medical attention. Another story commemorates a Turkish soldier. After the Australians tried to rush a line of the Turkish trenches, but were pushed back, this Turkish soldier saw a young Australian troop not too far from the Turkish trenches. The Aussie was rolling around on the ground, screaming for help. He lay there for about half an hour, screaming and yelling, so the Turkish soldier finally ripped some white cloth from something, then attached it to his bayonet on the end of his rifle. He waved it as a sign of peace and stood up from his trench, went out and picked up the Australian soldier, and carried him over to the Australian trenches so he could get medical attention. He then returned to his trench, and the two sides proceeded to fire at each other once again. By the end of the campaign, the ANZACs and the opposing Turkish troops had formed a deep respect for each other. General Ataturk, the commander of the Turks, said:

Those heroes that shed their blood and lost their lives ... You are now lying in the soil of a friendly country. Therefore rest in peace. There is no difference between the Johnnies and Mehmets to us where they lie side by side here in this country of ours.... You, the mothers, who sent their sons from far away countries, wipe away your tears; your sons are now lying in our bosom and are in peace. After having lost their lives on this land they have become our sons as well.

Turkey's ambassador to Australia, Tansu Okandan, said many countries had invaded Turkey in the past, "But only in one case have we allowed the foreign power to give its own name to a part of Turkey"—and that place is Anzac Cove.

With all that I had read and hear about Gallipoli, I couldn't shut up about how much I would love to go, and it would have been an awesome experience, more of a pilgrimage to pay homage rather than a trip. But the bottom line was the bottom line: I had ran out of money and would have to leave Gallipoli for hopefully another day sometime in the future. Nothing really more was said after that until we were walking home and I was chatting to Rob. Just then, out of the kindness of his heart, Rob gave me €100 to catch the bus and go down to Gallipoli for Anzac Day so I could pay my respects on our annual day of remembrance.

At first, I said, "No, I couldn't possibly accept this. I've had a long trip and it's time to work again."

Rob, though, said that he was just starting out and could afford to give me the money. "I really want to do this for you," he said.

"I'm not sure how I would repay you," I replied, "because I'll be on the road." Neither of us had mobile phones, and who knew when we would be in the same country again.

"You don't need to repay me," he said. "One day, you'll come across a situation where a fellow traveler will need your help in one way or another. So you should just pass on the karma and help them out as best you can. It's the way of the road. You are in need and I can help."

I stood there, feeling mesmerized. And so, thanks to this kind-hearted stranger who had no interest in seeing this place for himself, I went to Gallipoli for Anzac Day and got to pay my respects to our previous generations who laid down their lives for us and for future generations to come. Through the kindness of a stranger, the spirit of brotherhood and bonding lived on, just like the men who had lost their lives would have wanted from the future generations—to not discriminate because we were born in different lands. After all, as Abraham Lincoln supposedly alluded to, if we'd been born where they had been born, been taught what they'd been taught, we would believe what they believe.

To live in peace and tolerance, giving more than we take out of respect …

Lest we forget …

# CHAPTER 11

## LABOR IN VAIN

After arriving back in the UK, I stayed at the Drayton once again, this time for about a week. Louise had arrived there about eight days ahead of me, due to the fact that she had absolutely no interest in going to Gallipoli. She had even started doing a couple of part-time shifts at the Drayton, feeling quite comfortable jumping right back into the bar scene, considering her two travel friends were still working there.

Since I was in with the managers pretty good, they had no objection to me staying there, either. They even had a spare room at the time, so Louise and I slept there instead of crashing on a friend's floor. After a couple of weeks of freeloading (myself more than her), we managed to get a job in Stourbridge, just outside of Birmingham in the UK. I almost went alone, though, as Louise had a cousin near Bath and she said that she wanted to try to find work around there. But, considering the somewhat remote location of her cousin's one-street village town (where even the pub was quite a drive away), we decided we would stick together, visit them later, and go on to Stourbridge.

One of the best things about this next live-in job was that it would be off site. The boss had rented a house where he housed the staff. He had accommodations at the pub, but it was limited to the upstairs of one main living area where he and his girlfriend lived, another large area (where the head chef lived and I would eventually move into), and an office area.

The house was about a twenty-minute walk away from the pub, or a $5 taxi ride if you were feeling lazy. It was a typical terraced English house. The assistant chef,

114

Seb, lived on the first level. Ian, the assistant manager, lived in one of the two upstairs bedrooms, and Louise and I lived in the other. It was great to be living in a house, getting up and going to work five days a week, then being able to leave the pub and have our own space at the end of it—a definite novelty after living and working side by side with people for so long. Even though we were still living with a couple of the people we worked with, we had very little to do with Seb since he was in the kitchen, and Ian was never home.

Driving down the road for the first day of work from our accommodations, I specifically remember looking through the window of the car trying to spot the place we were going to be working. I finally thought I had found it, but as we drew closer and I could make out the sign, I realized it wasn't the right place. It was actually another pub just down the road, called the Labour in Vain. I remember thinking to myself that it might well be a sign of things to come—and it turned out that, except for the life experience and a bit of cash I got from the ten months there, it was indeed a portent of the future for me.

The pub was called the Three Pigs, and it was in one reasonably old building, probably dating back about two hundred years, so it had a lot of character. At the same time, though, it had also been reasonably kept up to the modern standards of interior décor, kind of a blend of the traditional and the new. Making it more unique was its three bars: a public bar, a back bar, and a restaurant bar.

Louise had been hired as a waitress to work in the restaurant, and I was to be the barman, sharing my time among all three of the bars. It was strange the way these three bars were all so close together but felt like totally different worlds. In the restaurant bar, the clientele were more of the up-market type, middle aged. They had money to spend, came for a meal, and didn't mind spending money to get the extra quality. The main bar was a hangout for the locals. There, we had four middle-aged fellows that always sat at the end of the bar. They had been somewhat successful in their life so far, came in every day, drank the same thing, and complained about the same thing. It was more of a working-class area, I guess you could say. It's also where we would get most of our walk-ins off of the street. Finally, the back bar was a hangout for some of the younger locals—the trouble-making crowd. Originally, we had a group of about five of them who would come in on Friday and Saturday nights, and they would get a little rowdy, but nothing out of the ordinary for a bar. At least, that's how it was when I started there. It would slowly degenerate into a bigger and bigger problem, though, and one I would eventually be responsible for dealing with. When we started working there, it was only a few weeks until Christmas, and obviously a busy time of the year. The place was fully staffed and doing a great turnover of money. We had five restaurant staff, as well as Kerry, the restaurant manageress—and the owner's girlfriend. Kerry had also started off as a member of staff herself a few months ago, before moving in with the owner Tony, who was about fifteen years older than she was. We also had four bar staff and a bar manager, as well as four kitchen crew.

But, as highly staffed as this sounds, when you consider that we had at most three bar staff on at one time, and considering the capacity of both the back bar and main public bar was about a hundred, something was missing … something lacking.

Fast-forward a couple of weeks later …

"Ugh, I don't have time for this!" Tony said one night at about 1:00 a.m.

"Time for what" I asked.

"To clean the bloody lines! I have to be up at 4:00 a.m. tomorrow."

"I'll do it for you," I replied.

116

He paused and looked at me with a furrowed brow. "You know how?" he asked.

"Yes."

It was another handy part of the job I had learned from previous positions. Although it had never specifically been my job to clean the lines, I went out of my way to lend a hand to learn it (oh, there might have also been a beer or two as incentive).

"Are you sure?" Tony asked.

"Yeah, mate, don't worry about it. I've got it."

He seemed hesitant at first, which was understandable, considering the chemicals used were corrosive and, although somewhat neutralized by the beer, if consumed by a customer … Well, the implications kind of speak for themselves.

Finally, he seemed to have at least a little peace of mind about it, maybe because of the air of confidence I was giving off and my usual straight-talking manner.

"Alrighty, then, that would be great," he said. "If you're 100 percent sure."

"Honestly, mate, I've done this many times before."

Still a little taken aback, he said, "Right, thanks." The he muttered, "Bloody Phil!" (Phil was the bar manager who had made his hundredth excuse for why he had to leave early to get out of doing work—because of his general lack of interest.)

"Mind if I drink the runoff?" I asked as Tony was walking away.

He laughed. "No. Go for it."

When you clean the beer lines on a tap system, a certain amount of beer is still in the lines, and it can't be put back into the keg. So instead of disconnecting the lines from the kegs and putting the cleaner through straightaway and ruining the beer in the lines, you can run water through the system to keep the beer drinkable. Depending on the length of the lines, you can get one to four pints per tap, henceforth free beer. At the Three Pigs, I knew it was about three pints per line. So with nine taps in the bar and three in the restaurant, that would make about thirty-six pints, more than enough for a merry evening with my coworkers.

So I started cleaning the lines and putting the runoff to one side until the rest of the staff were finished, then we all sat down to some free beer—which made me more than a hit with my coworkers, including the assistant manager Ian, who didn't know how to clean the lines.

It actually turned out to be quite an important night because Ian and I got talking. I had seen how bar was running, and had thought of a few improvements that could be made. I had suggested them to Phil, the bar manager, but they just seemed to fall on deaf ears. I didn't really take it any further after that because: First, I felt that if I did have something to say, I should be saying it to Phil, and if I was to go any higher, it would look like I was going behind his back. And, second, I didn't want to harp on it because people don't tend to take kindly to repetitive, albeit constructive, criticism.

But now Ian and I were sitting down enjoying some brews, and he seemed more than eager to listen. And what I was sharing wasn't anything really dramatic in terms of changing the business, just things like the way items should be stocked and rotated, or cleaning the lines on a more regular basis to keep the beer fresher, or encouraging the sales of "mixer" drinks—for example, a spirit mixed with a soft drink because that was where the biggest profit margins were. Ian seemed interested at the time, but once again, nothing really became of it. I came to see that Ian was the type of person who would feel insecure about his job if he approached Tony and gave him suggestions thought of by another member of staff. But these conversations did put in Ian's mind that I was interested in more than just the paycheck and that I had a few good ideas up my sleeve. So the next time that Phil decided to do a no-

118

show for work, Tony immediately fired him—and I got promoted to fill his position. My first bar manager job … just like that.

Of course, the new position had both good points and bad points. It definitely became a lot more interesting to go to work, as I had many other duties. I did the ordering of stock and also came up with promotional ideas. For example, the chef and I worked on Mars bar chocolate shots. These consisted of vodka infused with melted Mars bars, and it also worked well with Aero bars and a range of other goodies.

But I also certainly didn't like dealing with some of the bad things going on at the pub—especially things that Tony had implemented to try and make a quick buck. I remember when I first started working there, I thought it quite unusual that the drip trays (trays that sit under the beer taps to catch any excess) weren't dumped when they got full. I didn't think too much of it, though, because the excess was from bitter beers. Unlike lager, which is carbonated and henceforth will go flat very quickly, bitter beers have a slight carbonation, thanks to the liquid still fermenting with the hops in the cask. This means that the beer is constantly brewing, air is constantly being drawn into the keg, and it takes a lot longer to go flat. So I originally just presumed that they were using the beer from the drip trays in the beer batter for the fish and onion rings in the kitchen. It wasn't until later that I found out that bitter alcohol makes a pretty disgusting beer batter; it comes out all thick and doughy due to the lack of carbonation and active yeast in it.

What I eventually did find out, though, was after the place closed every night, Tony would come down, pull the drip trays, and then pour the contents back into the keg— not all of it, but over the life of a kilderkin keg (84-liter ale keg), he would put back about six liters, or twelve pints/serves, and into a firkin keg (42-liter ale keg), he'd

119

put back three liters or six pints/serves.

Although this doesn't really sound like much, it only took a little over three weeks to add up to another whole keg. Still, even though I didn't agree with this practice, I did it under Tony's orders, much to my discredit. Not only that, but my worst moment came one night when the two of us were talking and he made a sarcastic comment about how he wished he could do the same to the lagers (the more common carbonated beers), but knew he couldn't because, first, the flat lager would taint the rest of the beer in the keg; second, the lager system was pressurized by a mix gas of at about 30psi (almost the same as a car tire)—not enough to lose a hand, but more than enough to send suds flying everywhere; and finally, the couplings used to "tap" into the keg were designed to be tamper proof.

Ah, but given that I had a few beers in me already that night, and wanting to show off my "problem"-solving skills, I devised the following plan of attack. To get volume back into the beer without flattening it, I suggested using soda water, which was carbonated and basically free. I also recommended that we could de-pressurize the kegs by using a coupling without either of the two lines attached. By blocking off the top line (liquid outflow line), we could force any gas in the keg to escape back up the usual gas inflow line. With the pressure declining rather than increasing, the liquid would stay at the bottom while the excess gas escaped. Finally, by removing the small plastic ball/widget/one-way valve that sat in the coupling and normally prevented flow back up the gas line, we would have direct access to the beer as soon as it was de-pressurized.

Well, Tony reacted like a little kid at Christmas waking up to find a whole lot of presents under the tree. His eyes lit up as he stood up and said, "Bloody hell, you could very well be onto something here."

120

Instantly, I knew that I had only facilitated possibly adding to his dodgy activities. In my moment of drunkenness, I had a little moment of clarity and thought to myself how wrong this actually was—and how pissed off I would be if I spent my hard-earned money on something that should be so simple as a nice beer at the end of my hard day's work at the local pub, and it turned out to not be the quality my money had promised to pay for from the brewers. But there wasn't really much I could do now. I had set the ball rolling in Tony's mind.

The next day when I awoke, I thought about the night before with a little sense of worry, but tried to put it to the back of my mind and tell myself that Tony's enthusiasm had probably just been part of his drunkenness, and he would dismiss the idea altogether once he got going this morning.

But he didn't.

He called me into his office as soon as he saw me, which was midafternoon.

"Awright, mate," he said to me, using his usual greeting in his slightly posh Birmingham accent. "I've been onto this all mornin'. Couldn't bloody stop thinking about it." He let out in a cheeky little laugh, as he often did when he thought he was coming up with a brilliant idea or had been extra witty, laughing at his own smarts or jokes without a pause to see how other people would react.

Before I had a chance to respond, he said, "So hear me out. What I'm gonna do is do this for ya. Every stock-take, you're gonna get a cut from whatever excess we have in the literage from our beers. For example ..."

I listened as he proceeded to tell me his plan, all laid out like one of those mathematical riddles you have to solve in high school.

"At the start of a month, if I have ten barrels of beer, each forty-five liters, I have how many pints?" he asked.

"About nine hundred," I said.

"Right, so at the end of that month, if I have two barrels left, I have sold…?"

"Seven hundred twenty pints."

"Right. But, because of this new system I'm going to put in place, there should be a greater amount of pints sold. Let's say you get four more liters into a barrel. That's…?"

"Eight pints per barrel, sixty-four pints in total, with your registers saying 784 pints sold."

"Yep, so the profit on the excess will be…?"

"A hundred percent of 2.60 a pint, or 166.40 a month."

He smiled. "Exactly. Bloody hell! That took me an hour and a calculator to work out. Ha-ha-ha," he said, no doubt trying to flatter me a little so I would be more inclined to go along with his plan. "And of which, you will get a 50 percent cut—aaaand …" he said before I could say a word, "even though I'm already doing it, you will get a 50 percent cut from the bitters, so it's worth like an extra 300 quid a month to you. What do ya say?"

He must have seen the slightly negative look on my face, so once again, before I could react, he said, "Excellent, mate! Look, don't worry about it. It's all taken care of. I will do it most of the time, but you will have to do it occasionally. Just keep yer mouth shut, really. Ha-ha-ha. Just look at it like you're doing what your boss has told you to do."

When I didn't respond, he got up and said, "Right, I'm off to lunch. See ya later, Batman." (He would commonly and randomly refer to people like this.)

Before I knew it, he was out the door and I was left standing there, pondering what I had apparently just agreed to by my silence. It kind of hit me then that I had just been roped into some dodgy activities that I wasn't completely happy with—especially since they were my idea!

122

*What can I do?* I wondered, thinking it all through. *Well, I could report him.*

But I knew that would be worse than the act itself for me: going against and betraying someone who had been good to me, and who had given me not only employment and a place to live, but also opportunities to further myself. So I ruled that out as an option. My loyalty was too strong, even if it was a little illegal.

*I could tell him I want no part of it.* But then I thought I would lose the closeness we had developed together, and all future opportunities would pass me by because of it. Wasn't happy with that.

*I could quit and walk away.* But then Louise and I would both be out of a job and, once again, a place to stay. I knew neither of us would be happy with that, and being the time of year it was, it would have been hard to come across work in the industry. Plus, we would probably have to spend a fair bit of money that we didn't have to go back to square one and look for another job for the next few weeks to a month. That wasn't going to work.

*Or ... I could go along with it, play the somewhat devil's advocate, make a bit of extra cash. Don't have to do much besides keep my mouth shut and occasionally ...*

Well, I didn't want to go over it again and again in my mind. So then and there, I reluctantly decided that just going along with it was my best option, the easiest option, and it wasn't really going to hurt anyone in the long run. Kind of a white lie to myself, yes, but I figured it would keep the boss happy. And at the end of the day, for my peace of mind, I was going to do it under his orders. Well, at the time, that's how I ended up justifying it to myself anyway.

Fast-forward to several weeks later ...

It was time for a break, as we were well and truly past the slog of Christmas. By this time, I had settled into my new position quite well. It so happened that besides St.

Patrick's Day being only about ten days away, it was also Louise's birthday at the end of the month. So I decided to organize some time off Louise and myself, but to not tell her about it until the last minute. I had organized with Tony that we would take a week off, and to my surprise, everyone who knew about it managed to keep it a secret from her. She was under the impression that we were going to have our normal couple of days off. But when we woke up that morning of March 14, I told her to pack her stuff. She did, but she still didn't know where we were going.

"You know," I said when we got to the airport, "if it was up to me, I would blindfold you so you wouldn't know where we were going until we landed, but unfortunately airport security frowns upon people not being present at check-in and boarding plains blindfolded, so … we are going to Ireland for St. Patty's. Oh yeah, and happy birthday!"

Louise's jaw dropped and her eyes grew wide. "Awww!" she said, then, "Eek!" After that, she took a step forward, raised herself up on the tips of her toes, and gave me the biggest hug she possibly could. But then I could see a little bit of disappointment in her eyes, and it hit me that she must have been thinking that we only had our usual couple of days off.

"Oh yeah," I said. "I've got us a week off as well."

"But how?"

"I took care of it," I said.

"But where are we going to stay?"

I smiled. "I took care of it. Don't worry."

She quickly realized that all the logistics and planning had been taken care of. As all of this slowly sunk into her mind, it seemed to dawn on her that she could relax for the next week. This, then, would be our first normal, relaxing, pure, short, sweet, "package holiday" touristy experience.

Our first destination was Belfast, where we would

stay for two nights before catching a train to Dublin.

For me, the highlight of the trip was probably the Guinness factory in Dublin—a very unique place and not at all like the other breweries I had visited before. Basically, this factory was the very place where the Guinness brew had a humble beginning and then throughout the years had managed to stretch its corporate arms to most regions of the world. Many products like this obviously surround us in everyday life, but for some reason, I had never given it much thought—until I was standing at St. James's Gate, where this popular beer had been first brewed by Arthur Guinness 250 years ago.

Later, we went and saw the St. Paddy's Day parade, featuring all the color and culture that you would expect from the home of one of the most widely celebrated holidays in the world. We also got to see the beauty of Dublin's castle and learn about the tumultuous eight-hundred-year history held within its walls.

Unfortunately for us, by taking just a week off compared to the normal months we'd had before, it was over as quickly as the brief description in the last couple of paragraphs. Still, it was good to be away from the Three Pigs, and we had a more relaxing, pleasurable week than we'd even imagined before we left. Sometimes, it's not until you are outside a situation that you gain a different perspective on it, quite often for the better. And it would turn out that we'd need this holiday more than we realized at the time, because shit was really going to start hitting the fan when we got back.

# CHAPTER 12

## THE TWO WORLDS OF THE THREE PIGS

We arrived back to what could only be described as a shit show. Somehow, in the space of our week away, Ian, the assistant manager, had decided to quit. Apparently, he had ended up in tears because of all the pressure Kerry, the manageress, had put on him. When she got it in her mind that she didn't like someone, there was no hope for you. She would systematically and methodically do everything she could in her own snaking way to undermine you until you cracked and she got what she wanted, which in this case was getting rid of Ian. And even before we'd left, Kerry had been making sarcastic, snide comments about Ian, talk badly behind his back to customers and other staff, and she would even deliberately go out of her way to make sure he was under more pressure than necessary—and then push him further and further. To be honest, because I had seen this happening for a while, I wasn't really surprised. I had also heard how she had done it to a few other members of staff previously. It was just the way her acidic true personality was, like one of those stereotypical popular girls in school who is always the bully and putting everyone else down.

But Ian's departure did mean one thing in particular to me: the pub now had a position open for assistant manager. And lo and behold, it was offered to me straightaway. It seemed logical, I guess. I was already there, and I had shown good initiative and leadership, managing the bar. And most importantly, although not said out loud, Kerry and I got along to a certain extent. I definitely wouldn't say we were anything more than colleagues. We would never have a drink together after work or anything like that—unlike my relationship with Tony, who would regularly have a couple of pints with me. To Kerry, I think she mainly valued that I wasn't an idiot, that I couldn't be sucked in and manipulated by her. Oh, I let her think she had her own little bit of control in her own little way, but at the same time, she knew I wasn't one to be pushed over—and she knew that my opinions held sway with Tony.

I had never seen it in myself before, but apparently, a few people there had a great bit of faith in me—faith that I had a good aptitude for learning new things and being able to grasp the concept of most of it. Before long, I would be doing pretty much everything in the new assistant manager role, from helping Kerry run the restaurant to running the bar as well. Still, I was in a slightly awkward and limiting position. Although I was now helping out in the restaurant, Kerry's ego would never have allowed me to really have anything to do with running it. Still, I would lend a hand with just about everything happening in the restaurant: liaising with the chefs on the menus, making inquiries about and developing the wine lists more suited to the cuisine, doing the floats, balancing the tills ... I even kept the ball rolling with the expansion of different ideas and promotions to generate new business. For example, I decided to have a Saturday BBQ, during which I got on the barbie out in the beer garden and cooked steaks to order while also keeping a constant supply of grilled hot dogs going for anyone who felt a bit of the munchies coming on during football or whenever. But no way would Kerry let on to anyone that any of it wasn't part of her master plan, with me as the pawn and her behind the steering wheel of it all.

Over the next few months, I would learn even more about the "behind the scenes" aspect of the business: balancing the books, banking, paying wages, etc. I was soaking it all up and taking a lot of pressure off of Tony, which he was all too grateful for, even though he would rarely show it.

But with all this extra work piled on, it was getting a bit much for me, so I decided to hire a head barman and a couple of other staff to make the workload a little lighter and to help fill some gaps. I was also hoping to make everything a little more structured, with Kerry managing the restaurant (in theory, at least), someone managing the staff in the bar, and me going between both, managing the bar and picking up whatever slack Kerry was leaving in the restaurant—which was most everything, since she didn't want to do much besides boss around the staff and socialize with the customers. Now, don't get me wrong, Kerry was good at her job, and she was a lot more experienced than I. And, honestly, I learned a lot from her, but she was just over it. She didn't want to work. She would flutter in for twenty minutes, talk to some customers, order the staff around in spite of not knowing anything about the current situation in the restaurant (because she was never there long enough), and then disappear again.

It ended up being a tougher decision than you might think for me to hire a head barman because I realized I had to deal with an extra element that you wouldn't always come across. At that time, the drug scene in the back bar was slowly getting worse, and as it became more out of control, some violence started to creep in as well. Mainly, it revolved around one guy. Yes, we had know that some customers did a little bit of drugs before, and we knew it was common in this area, so Tony was willing to turn a blind eye to it. But things got a lot worse because of this guy Rick, who had recently been released from jail after serving time for drug charges.

Rick was in his early thirties, and sported a skin head and tattoos up and down his forearms. He had a solid build, and you could tell from the shifty look in his eye that he had been around, in a dodgy way.

The problems started getting out of hand when a group of about ten people in their twenties and thirties would make the back bar their haven from Friday night until Sunday night. They all knew each other and would come in after work on Friday, stay until we closed at midnight, go out to the nightclubs in Birmingham, and then be back at our place first thing Saturday morning at 10:00 a.m., still plenty high on drugs from the night before. They then proceeded to drink in the back bar all day Saturday, go out again Saturday night, and once again wander in Sunday morning, having not slept for two days. It was a bit of an amusement for all of us at first. These guys and girls seemed like machines. They would come in and occasionally be a little bit rowdy, but wouldn't do too much harm. They seemed to skip the come-downs by loading themselves with more booze and drugs. But when you wear yourself down like that weekend after weekend, it gradually takes its toll on you and becomes a bigger issue, which spills onto people around you.

Something had to be done, and unfortunately for me, Tony did not have the backbone for it and would cower at the first sign of trouble. So my thinking was that I would hire a guy with a bit of a rough attitude to hopefully be able to keep things down a bit. Unfortunately, one week into the new guy's employment, I caught him on the CCTV camera snorting coke with the locals off of a table in the back bar. I fired him immediately.

I felt in a way that I was becoming a joke to the regular customers in the back bar. They just didn't give a shit. And why would they? I was some twenty-year-old baby-faced kid from the other side of the world, managing the bar that most of them had been drinking at for at least four times longer than I had even been allowed to step foot into a pub. They soon started developing an attitude that it was their place, they ruled the roost, and they were putting money over the counter so they could do whatever the hell they wanted. By giving us their business, they were paying our wages, they figured. And Tony was never around to show his face and assert his authority because he was too scared.

And the more out of control the drug problem got in the back bar, the more violence came along with it. It wasn't long before we had at least a scuffle almost every weekend—and I would be the one to run and break it up. One time, I banned the group from coming back in again, and they went straight to Tony and convinced him to let them return. It was one of my many dilemmas. How was I supposed to have any authority in their eyes and have their respect out of fear of consequence when they could just go behind my back to the owner and twist things and circumstances to the way they wanted?

It was ridiculous.

So I went up to Tony and said, "How am I supposed to run a bar when I don't have your support?"

He said nothing, so I continued.

"These guys are fucking lowlife scum who think they can manipulate the staff at your bar to turn it into whatever kind of place they want, and it's driving away business—your business, your profit, your livelihood. What the fuck am I supposed to do, mate? You tell me. Why should I give a shit when you obviously don't?"

And with that, I walked away, slamming the door behind me. Tony did eventually come around, though it was a couple of days later. He actually came up to me and apologized, and said he finally realized how bad it had gotten.

"I'm behind you 100 percent. I will support whatever decision you make in there," he said to me in a genuinely enthusiastic manner.

Again, after pulling some teeth, I was getting somewhere. So I decided that I would again try to get some law and order in the place. The next time a fight happened,

130

I broke it up, grabbed both of the guys, and kicked them out, barring them for a month. The men were so disgusted with my decision that they went up to Tony the next day to plead their case, but this time, to my surprise, he actually backed me up. Although I had achieved what I wanted and gotten a point across, it pissed off more than a few of them, especially the ring leaders who thought they owned the place. So it wasn't long before tempers started to boil over—and they were aimed at me.

I was serving in the back bar just a couple of hours later when Rick came up to me and leaned over the bar. "Come here," he said in a manner and tone that implied he wanted me to lean closer so he could tell me something in confidence.

As I leaned in a little closer, he grabbed my tie with his left hand while cocking his right arm and clenching his fist.

"I could smash your fuckin' face in right now, kid," he said.

I said absolutely nothing. I just stared back at him, unblinking and unwavering in the face of his threats.

"One punch and I could change your face," Rick said. Then he turned and looked at his friend beside him. "Look at this fuckin' guy!" He looked back at me. "You're such a smug little fucker."

I just stared straight at him and said absolutely nothing.

"You're not even worth it" were the next words out of his mouth as he slowly released my tie.

I could see by the look in his eye that he knew his threats had fallen idly upon me, especially the way he'd started looking to his mate for support because his aggression just bounced right off of me.

I finished pouring a pint and left the bar. *Fuck me,* I thought to myself as I lit up a smoke. A wave of anger rushed over me and a level of fury kicked in as my pulse

131

raced higher and higher. But my thoughts weren't concerned with my well-being. I just couldn't believe that this guy thought he could completely disrespect me like that, right in the middle of the bar. The more I thought about it, the more enraged I became. I wanted to smack him in the face. I wanted to stomp on him. I was filled with the same rage that everyone is in situations like that when you look at them in hindsight. I wished I had just laid into him right then and there.

But I knew that it wouldn't have been a good idea. Besides, the way it would have looked (the manager getting into a fight), I knew that he would have absolutely kicked my arse. That was one of the reasons why I was able to stay so calm. I think I just switched off and was waiting for him to explode on me so I could quickly react and do whatever it would take to defend myself. But everything is different in hindsight. As I finished my cigarette, I knew one thing: I couldn't let him get away with that kind of treatment just like that. So I went back inside and walked straight up to him as he was laughing with his mates, probably about me and the situation.

"Can I speak to you for a second?" I asked as I looked at him with the same calm, stone-faced expression that I'd worn before with him.

He eyed me. "What the fuck you got to say?" he said. I honestly don't think he expected me to have the balls to confront him after what had just happened.

"Come on," I said as I turned away from him, then walked out of the bar and into the hall, which was somewhat secluded.

He followed along and looked at me.

"What are you doing?" I asked. "What was that supposed to be? Why does there have to be such a big problem? I'm here doing my job. I was hired to do a job and I'm doing it. Why is that such an issue for you?"

He stood there in stunned silence.

132

"Look," I said, "I know you're bloody drunk, but if you ever do something like that again, I'm going to ban you for life."

He just continued to stand there in silence. Without his mates to show off for, he didn't have much to say. So I walked off, hoping that would be the end of it.

While all of this was going, I had other problems creeping into my life. Louise definitely didn't take kindly to me being in management and telling her what to do. I could understand this. She was a very good waitress and was a hell of a lot better at that side of things than me, especially the whole social thing of relating to and flattering customers, as a host or hostess does as part of their role in the restaurant. Unfortunately, Kerry was still managing the restaurant when it pleased her, so there was no room for Louise to move up, which became very frustrating for her. And, because Kerry was hardly ever around, as mentioned before, I would quite often fill that role, meaning I would be ordering Louise around left, right, and center, which was hell on our relationship. We both knew that she was better at it, and I think because we were together, she felt that she could push back a little more against me, which undermined my authority with the other staff. A lot of the frustration that came out between us was because of Kerry, who had slowly taken a disliking to Louise, first because I think she felt a little bit threatened by Louise, and second because, with Ian gone, she'd grown bored and needed someone else to bully around. With the situation that I was in, who better to stir up than Louise to get a reaction out of both of us and watch some drama unfold, which Kerry devilishly thrived on?

It wasn't long before Louise got fed up and decided it was time for a change, which I did completely understand. We had been there for about five months by then, and in traveling terms, that was a long time. She had saved pretty good money and really didn't have to stay and be unhappy in that place. So she decided to go to Scotland, where she had a friend she'd first met working at the Drayton Court. She planned to stay there for about a month and do some work, just to experience something different and actually be somewhere she wanted to be, then come back and work with me again.

It worked out to be a nice little break for us. And, being that Edinburgh was only a couple of hours away on the train, she would come down and visit every second time she had days off, for starters. And after about four weeks of this, I took a whole week off and turned up on her doorstep to surprise her for four days off I had organized. But every time Louise came back to visit me, she would have a little run-in with Kerry and enjoy her time there less and less, especially being away from the friends she had now made in Scotland. Her visits became less and less frequent.

Now Tony, being the man he was (although sometimes he seemed to lack a pair), was by no means stupid in the conventional sense. I mean, at the end of the day, he did own his own business. He had made a fair bit of money in the past in the hospitality industry, drove the Land Rover, etc. In the business sense, yes, he was smart, but it was almost as if he had lost all enthusiasm for it. He just seemed like he didn't want to be there. And he was letting things with the bar and his personal life get out of hand. Kerry was a big part of it, as he knew. After all, she had started there as just another employee—a very attractive employee, if you get my drift. It wasn't long before their personal problems started spilling over on both sides, not just from Tony's lack of enthusiasm (due to being distracted by Kerry) but from Kerry herself. She didn't want to be there, and when she was, she liked to think that she ruled the world, which in her mind was Tony's establishment.

Kerry started getting more and more complaints about her personally and her attitude. It wasn't such a rare occasion that you would see her raise her voice to customers or even ask them to leave the restaurant because she didn't like their attitude, or even just sit at a table with some regular customers, ignoring all of the others while stating that she wasn't there to carry plates because she was the hostess.

Now, Kerry had left Tony before, normally over something like his jealousy toward her when she would flirt with customers or something along those lines, which was usually intentional on her part, to get back at him for something. But she would always come crawling back a couple of days later. She just couldn't stay away from the comfortable lifestyle that she had with Tony, spending all of his money and working part-time for it. She was definitely a gold digger in everyone's mind, but no one knew to what extent. Well, it was all about to unravel over the next few weeks.

It started one night after work. By this stage, I was living upstairs where the chef used to stay, as he had also quit in the past few months because of Kerry. It was an awesome room: one massive open area with a double bed, a big TV, a couch, drawers, closets, some gym equipment, a washer and dryer, and still a large amount of room to move around and spread out your things. Anyway, I was relaxing after work, drinking a few beers and playing some PlayStation, when I heard an argument break out from Kerry and Tony's accommodations, which were next door.

*What is it with bloody people who own bars and live and work together?* I thought.

It reminded me of working at the first bar again, as I heard intense shouting and then screaming, which I was all but happy to ignore—until I heard a large crashing sound of pots spilling over the floor.

*Bloody hell,* I thought. *They're gonna kill each other.*

All of a sudden, I heard the smashing of glass,

followed by a bloodcurdling scream—not one of horror or fear, but more one of complete loss of control, like someone had opened his or her very soul and was letting out all the buried frustration through one long, ear-piercing scream, which went through the whole neighborhood.

I rolled my eyes and grunted. *Better go have a look,* I thought as I put my beer down.

I headed toward their door and was thinking, *Should I kick it down if no one answers my knock?* It did sound pretty serious, after all. *Maybe I will just leave it be.* As I approached, though, I noticed that the door was slightly open. *Hmm. Damn. This could either be a good thing or a bad thing.*

I twisted a bit to the left to look through the crack in the door. I could see into their kitchen, and there was Tony with a bloody face—and Kerry wielding a hammer, threatening to kill him. (Luckily, Tony's sixteen-year-old son wasn't home that night, but was staying at his mother's.)

"What the fucking hell!" I yelled as I pushed open the door. "What the hell's going on?"

"She has bloody lost it!" Tony shouted. "She has finally flipped and gone mental."

Kerry looked absolutely irate. Plus, her face was swollen from tears and she had the look of a madman in her eyes as her mascara ran all over her face.

"I fucking hate him!" she yelled. "I fucking hate the world. I want to kill everybody in this fucking world—burn it all to the ground!"

I could see that her whole body was shaking uncontrollably as she shouted. She turned and swung the hammer at the oven and smashed the door, which shattered and further contributed to all the broken glass was already on the floor—thanks to the window she had smashed with the same hammer a few minutes before I arrived.

"The crazy bitch is trying to kill me!" Tony

136

shouted. "She bloody started on me for no reason—punched me right in the face."

"Whoa, whoa! Just calm down," I said, creeping closer to him. "And, Tony, please shut up. It's not the time to be calling her a 'crazy bitch' when she is wielding a hammer," I said, trying give the impression to Kerry that I was somewhat on her side so she hopefully wouldn't see me as a threat.

"You're just as bad, you little fuck!" she shouted with such strength that her voice cracked and began to give out, even as her head jerked from side to side. It looked like she was clenching every single muscle in her body, from the look of the veins bulging in her neck all the way to her toes, which were grappled together and covered in blood from treading on all of the glass in her bare feet—but she seemingly didn't notice. She moved closer toward me but, at the last second, turned to take a swing at Tony with the hammer. She was way too far away to hit him, but it did give me an opportunity to grab her arm and twist it to force her to let go of the hammer. It dropped to the ground with a thud on the wooden floor, echoing through the small room.

"Ha! You silly bitch, you fucking missed!" Tony said, bugging his eyes out at her.

Even in that moment, I recognized that he suddenly started feeling like a man because he wasn't alone and could now intimidate her. It drove her even wilder as she twisted her body and kicked him right in the shin, pulling her arm from my grip as she did so. She paused for a second until she realized that she was free, then she moved toward him. Kerry stood over Tony as he was bent over, rubbing his shin, and proceeded to punch and kick wildly at any part of his body she could manage to hit. I grabbed her from behind, then pulled her back and pinned her upper arms against my chest as I leaned backward to pull her weight away from him. She leaned back as well to try to get the maximum reach from her kicks that she was still planting into Tony.

"LET ... ME ... GOOOO!" she bellowed in a deep, threatening voice.

As she yelled, Kerry threw her head back and struck my chin. I pulled her arms tighter behind her back so as to hurt her a little.

"Don't you fucking do that again," I said. "I'm trying to help."

"Get your fucking hands off of me!" she yelled. "You can't touch me. Who the fuck do you think you are?"

Now she turned more of her attention toward me, getting more violent with backward kicks to my shins and attempted rearward head-butts.

"I'm bloody warning you," I said, but she wouldn't stop. "Right, that's it!"

I leaned farther back to pick her up off the floor. Then I twisted my body and slammed her onto the ground. She was so irate that it didn't even seem to affect her in the slightest. As my body followed hers onto the floor, I let go of one of her arms, then twisted them both behind her back and put my foot into her neck, trying to keep her still.

"I'm calling the police on this, crazy bitch," Tony said.

"Good idea," I said as I noticed blood running down my cheek from one of her head-butts.

It took all of my strength to keep her pinned down on the floor. She was clearly on coke or something. Finally, after what seemed like forever, the police arrived, cuffed her, and took her away.

Tony really didn't have much to say to me after they had taken her away, not even a "Thank you," actually—just a few snide comments about how crazy she was and how he'd had enough and wasn't going to let her back. I had heard this a few times before, though, and as much as I hoped that it would be true (not only for my state of mind, but also for the business's success, and for Tony

138

and his son), I had my doubts.

I didn't really see Tony for a couple of days after that, until I noticed about six suitcases at the bottom of the stairs.

"What's going on?" I asked him.

"It's all her stuff," he said. "I was serious, mate. That bitch has been bleeding me dry for a long time now and she is done. Her friend is coming to get her things. I won't even let her near the place anymore. And as for you, I want you to be my general manager. I'm going to teach you everything, and you will have the full run of this place. You're a very smart man and good at your job. I'm going to be there to guide you, but what I want in twelve months is to be able to walk away from this place and have you running it for me. What do you say?"

"Right-o." It was the only response I could come up with after such an out-of-the-blue proposal.

# CHAPTER 13

## MOTHER HEN AND HER GAGGLE

So it was time to step up again. Tony had kicked Kerry out, and she was really and truly out of the picture—no more meddling, no more of her facetious ways to deal with. A weight off of everybody's shoulders …

And I was the new general manager. Tony didn't want to have anything directly to do with the place except when he was needed, mainly because of all of the personal things he had going on in his life. I was to be in charge of everything, from the hiring and firing to overseeing the kitchen, restaurant, and bars. Even I knew that it was a mighty position for a twenty-year-old to have.

Over the course of the next month, I realized just how much Kerry had been sucking out of the place. For instance, I noticed that although Tony had been watering down the beer, we were somehow still down in our stock, which seemed impossible. After doing some investigating of the account books (which I hadn't had access to before), I realized that someone had been refunding excess pints into the register—refunding beers and large quantities of types we didn't even stock anymore—then taking the excess money out. Sometimes Kerry wouldn't even bother trying to make it look legitimate, as our tills would be £50-£150 down at the end of some days. She would just steal the money outright. It all mysteriously stopped when she left, or course.

The first time I came to calculate the tips, I also noticed a massive difference. For instance, during the busy Christmas period, we would get maybe an extra £30 a week, which was twice a normal week. Then, after Kerry had left and I was calculating tips, it worked out that each member of staff received about £60 on a regular week, both restaurant and kitchen staff alike. Thus, I calculated she was stealing about £300 from staff tips every week.

Things were changing all around, though, so it was time to move on from all of that. Tony decided that he wanted to do some renovations as well. So we closed the restaurant for a week, rented some equipment, and I spent my days sanding back the floors and repainting the restaurant, skills that I had learned in previous jobs or learned on the fly now. The restaurant opened again for business, and life on that side was back to normal. We were back in full swing, serving old customers and new, good customers and those not so good—those occasional annoying know-it-all asshole kind of customers to be more precise.

Most people who have worked in the restaurant industry will know the type I am talking about when I describe the next group of people. They've always been around and always will. It's the group that is led and spurred on by that one person—the one that acts as if, in previous generations, his or her family had money and were part of the "elite," so to speak, but now just lived the average financial existence: have a mortgage, a couple of kids, etc. Nothing wrong with that, but they have a snobbish attitude toward servers, as if they are some sort of seventeenth-century slave s, and these people go out of their way to prove that they are better and more knowledgeable than you about your job. This, of course, is the highlight of their otherwise boring lives, when they make it out once a month, crew in tow.

Well, when the restaurant was a little quiet early in the week, we had one of these groups come in one evening. We had maybe half a dozen tables open of the twenty-three in the restaurant. I had someone working in the public bar, and I was working in the restaurant with a young waitress (sixteen years old), named Gill. As these people walked in together, I could tell straightaway they were "that" kind of group. The "mother hen," as I'll call her, led her flock into the restaurant, extravagantly waving her arms about, trying to attract attention to herself as she ever so loudly made her entrance while finishing off her story about some trip she had taken down to the Lake District as all the others oohed and ahhed at their leader.

They made their way to the restaurant bar, and as they all gathered around, I said, "Good evening. How are you?"

No one replied until they had all taken a good, hard look at me and the restaurant, no doubt to see if we would meet with their approval.

"Ahhhh, yes," Mother Hen said. "Good evening to you as well ... young man."

I could almost feel the condescension dripping from her every word.

She smiled. "And I see I will have to take care of the wine selection tonight, being that I very well could be ordering a bottle that was born in the same year as your waitress here." Then she started to laugh, and her gaggle joined in her cackling a few seconds later.

Gill squirmed a little, as I could sense that she felt insulted by the comment.

"Well, you won't have to worry about that," I said. "We do have a regular wine-tasting for all our front-house employees, which includes suggestions on why a wine may complement a dish or not, so she is quite clued up."

"Ah, yes, looks can be deceiving, can't they?" Hen said.

Though I didn't show it, I immediately took a distaste to her.

Meanwhile, the poor young waitress Gill was standing beside her, nervously waiting to show them to their table. I looked at her as if to say, "Don't worry about her. She's one of those."

142

"If you would like to be seated, Gill here will show you to your table and bring you some menus" was my only reply, though. I bit my tongue, as you often have to do in the industry.

I would have offered them a drink at the bar first, as I usually do, but I honestly didn't want them hanging around. I just wanted them in their seats having a conversation amongst themselves and not disturbing or antagonizing anyone else. Unfortunately, though, this wouldn't be the case. Every five minutes or so, Mother Hen would call for Gill to come over so she could throw her weight around a little and show off to her gaggle. Unlike Gill, I myself had met these types of customers many times before, and they were all the same, led by the ring leader— the ones who show off to the group, orders the wine, makes recommendations on the menu even though they have never had it before (only read about it), and think they have some kind of expertise because they have eaten out in a restaurant once a month for the past twenty years and once did a two-week trip to France or Italy, which of course made them quite the expert on French wine and Italian cuisine. They assume dominance in their group and then they try to assume it over the whole restaurant by trying to make their table the center of all attention for the staff.

This ridiculous pestering of Gill by Mother Hen continued for quite a while. It ranged from everything like a snide comment about the décor to asking in-depth information about the chef—and even impossible questions about the wine, like "How do you think the tannins in this wine affect the nuttiness of the wine over the extra two years this is kept in the cask before bottled, compared to one, say, from the southernmost region of Chile, high in the Andes? Do you think maybe the altitude affects it?" This was obviously something she'd read somewhere and was now misquoting, as you could tell she was not a connoisseur and had definitely never been to the Andes

143

before.

I noticed Gill becoming more and more frustrated with these people every time she walked past me, but she would never say anything because she was way too polite to complain and, being only sixteen as well, was a little shy. So I decided to take over waiting on the table and told her to go about other things.

Immediately, Mother Hen took notice and couldn't help herself: "Oh, now we have moved from someone in preschool to someone in high school serving us. Oh, what a treat."

A couple of the ladies kept their mouths shut, probably because they knew how rude she was being, while a couple of others laughed only out of support for their friend.

"Ah, yes. Well, I guess we must have graduated in the same year," I replied, winking at one of the other ladies who was keeping to herself out of embarrassment. I thought giving Mother Hen a compliment would help settle her down a bit (she was about fifty years old). Although she was silenced for a moment, as she wasn't expecting such a response, it didn't keep her from carrying on the way she had. Even the people at a table close by kept looking over and rolling their eyes at her attitude.

Soon enough, Mother Hen requested to speak to the chef so she could ask him about the food. I agreed, just to keep her quiet. Seth, whom I had lived with at the house, was the acting head chef that night. I explained the situation to him and asked him to come out. I didn't leave the table, though, as I wanted to hear every word.

Questions of a ridiculous caliber ensued:

"Where is this beef from—not what butcher, but what farm?"

"Why is this jus so sweet? When I make it, it's not sickly sweet like this."

"What do you do to the vegetables to make them

like this? I bet it isn't healthy for you."

The interrogation continued for about a minute and then I said to Seth, "You must be busy, mate. Better get back in the kitchen."

Mother Hen shook her head. "Naïve little restaurant with naïve little people," she said, looking each one of her group in the eye.

And with that, I walked away, saying nothing. I went to the bar and returned to the table with Gill and three corks.

"Clear the table," I whispered to Gill.

As she proceeded to bus the table, I handed the three corks to Mother Hen.

"Here you go," I said.

She pulled her head back a bit and looked at me with a furrowed brow. "What are these for?" she asked.

"To put in your wine bottles," I replied, "because you are now leaving. You have been rude to every member of our staff and have been making the other customers feel uncomfortable for a long time now. I want you to leave."

Now her eyes got big. "What! Who do you think you are? I want to speak to whoever is in charge!"

"I am in charge," I said.

"I want to speak to the restaurant manager, then."

I shook my head. "He's not here tonight, and when he is, he answers to me. I am the general manager, and the buck stops with me—and I am asking you to leave."

"But we haven't finished our meals."

"That's okay. I don't expect you to pay for it. Just pay for the wine … because I know that you enjoyed the lovely taste of the tannins that were present throughout," I said, hoping the sarcasm would not be lost on her—and it wasn't.

"Ha-ha-ha." She stood, cocked her head back, and smiled as she looked down her nose at me. "Don't be silly, boy. I should have know that you wouldn't have know that tannins are only found in red wine. It's because the white wine isn't distilled long enough for them to be extracted from the grape skin. That's why you only have that taste in red wine."

"Actually, no," I replied, trying not to get too excited that she had walked straight into my trap. "Tannins come from all grape skins, yes, but it's not because of the age difference between most red and white wines as to why there are originally very few in white wine. It is because of the difference in the fermentation process. White grapes are pressed to extract the juice before the fermentation process takes places, giving it less time in contact with the skin and seeds, where the tannins are extracted from—unlike red wine, which is fermented in the skin.

"But besides that, there are also detectable tannins in your white wine. You see, a tannin is a naturally occurring polyphenol found in plants, seeds, bark, wood, leaves, and fruit skins. So although you don't get any from the grapes, as it is aged in a wooden cask—specifically being oak in that chardonnay you are drinking—that's where the tannins are extracted form. So you see, on the label when it describes your wine as having a vanilla taste, that is because the functional group of tannin or polyphenol that is extracted from the oak barrel is vanillin. And the vanillin gives it that vanilla taste described in that description there."

And with that, there was nothing left to say. Mother Hen pulled out more than enough cash to cover the wine, left it on the table while saying absolutely nothing and not making eye contact, and then she led everyone out, never to return again.

Gill had the biggest grin on her face for the rest of the night, and compliments from other customers abounded as everyone praised my handling of the situation—with many insisting on buying me a drink.

# CHAPTER 14

## FIGHT NIGHT

Things were going well over the past month or so, and with Kerry out of the way, Louise wanted to come back and live there again—not to work, as we knew that hadn't gone well, but just so we could live together and see each other more regularly. We had missed each other quite a lot, but things just weren't going to be that easy. We had a regular in the bar named Giles. He was in his midforties and had been drinking in the place for twenty-odd years. He had talked with me about buying the place a couple of times and had casually asked me not to say anything to Tony. But one night when I was drunk, I accidentally let it slip to Tony—and being the greedy guy that he was, Tony didn't want to wait for an offer to come through the proper channels; he wanted to hear a price straight from the horse's mouth. So he approached Giles about it. And, naturally, Giles was furious that I had told Tony. I tried to apologize but Giles wouldn't have any of it. So, to get his revenge, he told Louise that I had been sleeping with one of the bar maids while she was away. To my surprise, Louise believed him!

Louise had seen how I'd been attracted to the bar maid and how she flirted with me, and Louise had thought that she would try to make a move as soon as she was out of there. I don't know why, but she never really trusted me in that sense, even though I'd never gave her a reason not to. Maybe it was because she had been cheated on in the past, or maybe it was because more than a few times I'd stayed out drinking with groups of predominately girls while we were on the Greek islands, after Louise had gone to bed—and with mutual friends of ours, as well, though always with her permission. Maybe it was the reputation I had when we'd first met at the Drayton Court. Personally, I felt that while we were together, I had given her 100 percent of my love and attention, and always considered and respected her feelings in that way. Still, she'd gotten it in her mind that I wasn't one to be trusted.

"Why would Giles lie to me?" she asked me. "What possible reason would he have to make up a story like that?"

I tried to explain to her that he was trying to get revenge, but when she confronted him about it, he denied ever making an offer to Tony to buy the place. She didn't even bother to ask Tony because she didn't trust him, either, and thought he would just lie to cover for me. So just like that, her moving back was put off. Oh well …

We were starting to get more repeat customers in the restaurant, and for the most part, they were passing on positive news about the place to their friends. The stock take was balancing out, and the tills were correct for the most part, taking into account the occasional human error. Well, of course they were right when we had one less thief working there. But there was still one major concern, and that was the back bar. And that all came to a head on one Saturday night.

The usual group had been drinking for over twenty-four hours and were off their nuts on drugs and alcohol. Once again, things were getting rowdy in the back bar and overly heated. It turned out that a few days before, one of the guys had found out that one of his friends had been sleeping with his girlfriend. I didn't know it just then, but things were about to explode.

Luckily, it was fairly late in the evening, and things were winding down in the restaurant, even though it had been busy earlier on, but now we didn't have a lot of later bookings.

I was in the restaurant bar at the time, when all of a

148

sudden, I heard yelling and screaming and carrying on in the hallway just around the corner from me, near the back bar's entrance. I came out to investigate and saw a jumbled mess of bodies. Two main guys were obviously trying to go for each other and a few other people tried to hold each of them back. Then the one guy yelled out, "You're a fucking slut!" It was aimed at the girlfriend who had cheated on him. This, of course, contributed to the escalation of the situation, as the brother of that girl was also a regular in the bar and he didn't take kindly to his sister being called a "slut," obviously. So he also decided to jump in and have a go at this guy.

At that stage, I also decided to jump in the middle, as I felt obligated to break it up.

"What the fuck are you guys doing?" I shouted. "Chill the fuck out, the lot of you!"

I got between the now three main guys and turned my attention toward the two guys who were after the one.

"Relax," I said in a somewhat calm voice. "Chill the fuck out. Piss off outside if you're going to cause shit. Now … just relax. What's the bloody problem?"

Right then, a couple of other guys stepped in and helped to separate the guys a bit more—not out of respect for me or the establishment, obviously, but because of the thought that their mates might get barred from the place, as they knew I had been clamping down more and more on this kind of behavior.

The guy in the line of fire was dragged toward the door by his mates, and he was now out of sight to the others, so he decided to turn his abuse toward me.

"You're a little fucking bastard as well," he said to me.

"What was that?" I asked.

"You can go fucking fuck yourself, you wanker. Get the fuck out of my country, you convict poof."

That was when I decided I'd had enough—enough

149

of the abuse, enough of the arguments, enough of the hatred toward me for just doing my job.

"Get the fuck out of here and don't come back!" I yelled. "You're fucking barred."

Now this wasn't the first time I had barred this guy. Recently, I had barred him for a week for snorting up coke in the toilets.

"You're out of here this time and you're not coming back!" I said.

And with those comments, the guy went absolutely irate, and for some reason (quite possibly because of his drug-induced state), he immediately turned his abuse back on the guy who was the brother of his girlfriend, even though he was around the corner out of view.

"I'm gonna fuck you up, John!" he said.

"I'm waiting for you. Bring it on. I'll have you and your little slut sister."

Now this area of Birmingham was known as being a little bit rough. It was home to the local football hooligans, and not just in this bar. There were regularly fights just up the road and down the high street. They were the type of guys who for some reason thought they had to prove how hard they were and would do so if given even the slightest excuse to.

I actually thought that John had managed to be quite reserved, even after they'd hurled abuse at him for the past ten minutes now. Although John's mates were holding him back, I could tell he wasn't acting up and defending himself as much as most people in that situation normally would. I presumed that maybe he had a little bit of a guilty conscience about everything.

Just as these thoughts passed through my mind, who else but John came barreling around the corner, yelling, "Let's go, you little fuck!"

With both of them still inside the establishment, I didn't want anything to happen, so I stood in the middle of the hallway as he came charging toward me.

"Don't do it!" I yelled. "I'm warning you!"

He didn't even make eye contact with me; he pushed straight past, laying his shoulder into me as he went, knocking me into the wall as he rushed past and then tackled the other guy, forcing the whole scene spill out into the street.

This was enough to really piss me off now. So even though it was outside of the place, I proceeded to go outside and rip the guy off of the other who had pushed past me, throwing him farther down the pavement.

I remember standing there and saying "You're fucking out of here for good, asshole!" as he looked up at me, unsure as to what had just happen. Right then, about ten other people came pouring out of the bar, all pissed off and all looking for a bit of action.

They guy whom I had thrown to the floor got up at this stage and proceeded to go for the guy whom he had originally knocked on to the ground—or so I thought was the case. As he cocked his arm getting ready to punch at him, at the very last second he turned his attention to me and sucker-punched me straight in the face. I took one ... two steps backward ... and with that, I straightened my posture since he had managed to make me sway backward with the punch.

I looked him dead in the eye and said, "Is that all you got, you little fuck?" and then let out a cheeky little laugh.

He backed off immediately, clearly surprised that I had taken the punch so well.

Now about eighteen people were outside, many of whom had come to join in. It quickly turned from a little scuffle into a brawl. It was to unclear who was on whose side, but I did know that none of them were on mine. I tried to stay on the outside of the fight as much as possible, as I thought that I could have about five guys on me at any stage. Although the fight had originally had nothing to do with me, I knew that more than a few people who would have loved nothing more than to throw a cheeky punch my way.

About four different fights arouse now, mostly one-on-one, but there were a few sucker-punches thrown here and there when people weren't looking, and a couple of two-on-ones if someone's mate started losing a fight. Then one fight, which looked more like an intense vertical wrestling match, started to come my way. I backed up slowly and was soon on the other side of the road, as the brawl now consumed not just the pavement in front of the bar, but the whole road.

All of a sudden the guy who had sucker-punched me appeared from behind the group and tried to sucker-punch me again. Although he was quick and came out of nowhere, this time I saw him coming and managed to drop my chin so he hit the hard crown part of my head. He clearly hurt his knuckles punching me there, more than he'd hurt my head. His next move was to square up to me, so I slipped in one quick left jab straight between his raised fists, knocking him onto his ass and stunning him.

Then another guy from the group fighting near me broke away and also came toward me. He swung for me, and as I blocked it, he threw his arms up as if to say that he didn't want to fight, or maybe that he didn't realize it was me, but it didn't matter. I didn't care at this stage. He had swung at me and that was it. He knew what he was doing. As I went forward toward him, he lunged his whole body at me, as if to tackle me. I twisted my body around and got him in a headlock, and he got in a quick little punch at my cheek on his way down.

I didn't really want to strike him when he was in the headlock, so I dragged him over on to the pavement and rammed his head up against the fence as if to give him a warning. He got the point, and I let him go. He ran away.

The fight was finally starting to die down at this stage and people were separating.

I stood there and yelled, "I know every one of your faces. I've been here for the whole thing. You're not going to carry on like this here anymore. I've given you chances time and time again. You're barred, the lot of you. Now piss off and never come back!"

And with that, they started to slowly disperse. They had let out their anger on each other, then realized that they were fighting the same guys they drank with night after night and were also friends with. They had come to their senses, it seemed.

I stood there, watching them leave, still infuriated by the whole situation. And as I watched, I looked up and saw Tony standing in the window. He had been there watching the whole thing, never having the balls to come down or even yell out the window. But what more did I expect? He was a coward focused on only his own interests, but I couldn't hold that against him, really. My opinion of him was changing more and more. Even though he had given me so many opportunities in the business, my respect for him was starting to falter. He was a crook. I was giving him my all and wasn't getting much return, besides the experience I gained for myself. The respect and care he had for me were confirmed two weeks later when it was my twenty-first birthday. After all I had done for him, his only gift was £21—not even a card, just a last-minute gift of £21.

That night of the fight, though, was a big turning point in the way the bar did business. I had gotten rid of all of the scum from the back bar. Yes, business died down at first due to the half a dozen troublemakers I had banned, along with a few of their loyal friends who didn't want to drink there anymore because of it. But it only took a few weekends before business started to pick up. We were getting a more respectful crowd, and not only that, but they

153

were spending more money because they weren't on so many drugs all of the time. But it wasn't too long before, once again, this place had a big surprise for me. About a month later, I woke up one morning to find Kerry walking around upstairs.

"Hello, Adam, darling. How are you?" she said. "Great news. Tony and I are back together."

And with that, Kerry moved back in, although Tony proclaimed she wouldn't have anything to do with the business. Still, it didn't take long for her to start being facetious in other ways. Louise came back again for a visit, and Kerry started intimidating her right off. I knew it was indirectly aimed at me, though. Kerry couldn't have me around, as she knew that I knew all of her little secrets about stealing, etc. And although I never said anything to anyone else besides Tony about it, she had it in her mind that I had been slagging her off to the customers, telling them everything about her. She became paranoid as to why customers were acting strangely toward her, and that was the conclusion she drew—when in actual fact, they were acting that way because they had seen all the drama unfold with her for themselves, and, well, Tony had to give some explanation as to why she'd moved out.

About a week after Kerry moved back in, her snideness toward me started back up. She would make her way through the restaurant and bad-mouth me behind my back, saying various things about me to undermine me and my authority. She went back to exactly the way she had been before. Tony didn't look me in the eye for weeks. He knew what I thought, and things were coming to a head once again. I simply couldn't work like this. Kerry was clearly on a mission to push me over the edge. I even heard from a regular customer that she admitted to asking a few of her friends to come in on different occasions and complain about me and the service I was giving—just so she could get rid of me and once again not only to be in

154

control of the place, but also to be able to manipulate the stock and tips so she could gain an income from it. Because she was so lazy, she didn't want to really work, just freeload.

The second time Louise came for a visit after Kerry's return, the two of them had some sort of argument and Louise came storming into my room.

"Ugh! I hate her!" Louise said. "She is a nasty, backstabbing, two-faced bitch." These were pretty strong words for Louise, normally a fairly placid person who mostly would rather let an argument go than be involved in it.

"What did she do?" I asked.

"It's just everything. It's the way she is. You know what sort of person she is and how she gets under your skin. She just makes it her mission to make your life hell. She is a bitch—and I told her so. She didn't like that very much, but I'm not sorry."

I smiled and laughed.

"I'm packing my things right now and going back to Scotland," she said and looked at me. "She has barred me from the place."

"What! You're kidding. She can't do that!"

"Well, she did."

I immediately walked out and knocked on Tony's door to speak to both Kerry and Tony.

"So what's going on?" I asked.

Kerry jumped in straightaway with "Oh, you don't need her, Adam. You can do so much better. She is an insecure little bitch and—"

At this point, Tony cut her off, which took us both by surprise, considering the sort of person he was: "Look, there is nothing I can do," he said to me. "Obviously, our women can't and won't get along, and this is the one I have to live with. I'm sorry if she doesn't want her here, but she is just going to make my life hell otherwise."

155

"What am I supposed to do?" I said to Tony. "Do you see what kind of position she has put me in? Kerry refuses to let her be here in peace, and not even to work here again, but just to stay here on her days off while she's visiting me. Where does that leave me?"

"I know," Tony replied.

"Well, I'm not going to be in this miserable situation, not being able to have my girlfriend visit and having to watch while Kerry weans her way back in and kills the business again. I'm going to have to leave."

And with that, I verbally gave my resignation of two weeks. And two weeks later, I was in Scotland with Louise.

///////

I had been staying with Louise a few days in Scotland. Our relationship still felt a bit rocky, but we had decided to give it a little more time to see if it would work itself out. Louise, though, was over Edinburgh, and due to the lack of live-in positions ( Louise had an apartment, was working in a bar, and wasn't able to save any money), we decided to try for somewhere else after having a little break. She still had about five weeks left on her lease (another downfall of an apartment) and wasn't about to give up her deposit, so we decided that after her lease was up, we would go to Bath, where her cousin Jay lived, and maybe go from there. She also liked the idea of being a little closer to family. But I wasn't about to just hang around Edinburgh for five weeks, so I started thinking, *I've been working for about a year and have some pretty good coin saved up. What a perfect time for an adventure.*

Almost immediately, the Great Pyramid of Giza came to mind—the oldest Wonder of the Ancient World and the only still remaining mostly intact, almost five thousand years old, and something that had fascinated me since childhood. Plus, it was a site that 50 percent of avid travelers visited, so we agreed on a plan. Louise would finish her time in Scotland, and I would be off on an adventure and then meet up with her five to seven weeks later at her cousin's place in Bath.

# CHAPTER 15

## ANCIENT CIVILIZATIONS

Although I loved traveling with Louise, I learned a long time ago that you can never wait for people in life if it means you are missing out on your own. She couldn't/didn't want to come, and I wasn't going to let that stop me. In fact, I'm pretty sure I wouldn't have traveled to Egypt if we had been on a trip together, so in a way, it was meant to be. I knew then and still know now that if I had waited for someone to travel with over all the years, I would never have been able to see and do half of the things that I managed to.

Growing up, I had always been fascinated by the Middle East and Africa. No matter what had transpired anywhere throughout the history of humanity, this was where it all began. Everyone from every corner of the globe originated on this mother continent. I remember sitting in the plane at the window seat as I was arriving at the Cairo airport, looking out as the plane was about to touch down. The plane hovered above the ground for a few seconds before making a thud on the tarmac. I thought, *Welcome home. Here for the first time but probably not the last.* I was the closest to the beginning of everything that I had ever been, where my existence could be attributed to coming from if you traced back the lineage far enough.

I was looking forward to exploring the ancient pyramids of Egypt, and beyond that, who knew where I would end up. That's what made it so exciting. I had a goal in mind, but after that, I was open to anything. The road was my oyster, so to speak.

I recalled in my mind what we as kids growing up in Australia had been taught by our parents, our teachers, and the media about the sort of place the Middle East was: a place of turmoil and struggle, it basically boiled down to. It was apparently inhabited by people who just couldn't let go of the past, a people who couldn't understand the value of human life and how we could all live in peace together if we just made a little effort. People were spurred to believe there are differences between us because of religion—apparently, people less educated and less wise than us. But I knew that there are always two sides to every coin, and I was looking forward to exploring the culture of the people and history of the region for myself, and then forming my own opinions.

My first stop, then, would be Cairo. The first place I stayed was a rundown old shell of a hotel, at which most people would have turned up their noses, let alone pay good money to stay there (although it was only a couple of dollars a night). But to me, it had a kind of character to it, a sense of its own history that was rare to me growing up in such a young country like Australia.

I had decided to stay in a hotel rather than a hostel because Egypt didn't really have many hostels. There was no real need, either, since the hotel prices were so low. This was okay, though, because it meant that all backpackers stayed in hotels, so I still had the social aspect of it, while having the privacy of my own room.

One thing that took me by surprise besides the décor of the hotel were the armed guards on duty in front of the hotel. And it turned out that it wasn't just the hotels that had a heavily guarded presence. I saw it all around the city. I learned that these were special "tourist" police who were there to protect the tourists, as the name implies. It wasn't out of some kind of honorable gesture to nobly protect people who had decided to come and visit from far away, but more to stop an incident happening for Egypt's own benefit, to keep money coming in because the nation's economy was largely based around tourism.

At the hotel where I was staying, I heard from a few other travelers that there were a couple of places in the city where someone could get a fake student card. With this card, you could get discounts up to 60 percent off historical sites, transportation, and attractions around the world for as long as it was valid. So, obviously, I decided to try to get one. I went to the office, filled out the paperwork , wrote down my school (the BS University of South Australia— I'm sure you can figure out what the BS stands for), what I was studying (future history—specializing in the evolution of humanity from our current state to that of Jedi knights), and so on and so forth. One hour later, I had my fake ID/money-saving card.

Egypt ended up being different from any country I had traveled to before. In the areas I explored, it was common to see buildings that were run down, degraded, and falling apart. There seemed to be a massive lack of road rules as well, with people ignoring what most people in the West would just call common sense: not indicating, not giving way … just a complete jumbled mess. But somehow this entropy of traffic ticked along and got people where they needed to go, most of the time in a safe manner. Still, I did see a couple of crashes during my time there. In any case, I always seemed to find a surprise around every corner when navigating my way through Cairo.

I was even surprised by the pyramids while I was intentionally on my way to see them. I was on a bus in the sprawling outskirts of Cairo when, all of a sudden in the background, I saw the peak of a pyramid in the distance. It just arose out of seemingly nowhere, right there amidst the modern-day junk architecture. It was strange to think that in all this revelry of commuting with the incessant honking of car horns and motorbikes zooming by, weaving in and out of pedestrians, that not far away sat something so ancient and magnificent. I sometimes wondered if the people of Cairo even knew that the pyramids were there—or maybe they weren't. Maybe they were just a figment of an adventurous spirit and imagination? I eventually arrived somehow after catching those local buses, with me not speaking any Egyptian and using hand signs and pointing at words of places I had highlighted in my travel guide, giving money and hoping it was enough, wondering when my stop would be and hoping not to get lost.

I remember finally getting there and walking about 300m toward the Sphinx. Memories of an old photograph I had seen came to my mind: a photograph of Australian troops during World War II sitting on the sphinx. I don't know why this image came to my mind, but when it did, it reminded me of how timeless this piece of human history was. It was mind blowing to ponder the millions and millions of people this statue must have seen over the thousands of years it had been standing. To think what possible thoughts could have gone through those people's minds as they looked upon the same thing as I. To think of the famous people who had stood in the same spot as me and stared right back into the eyes of the half-man half-lion that guarded the pyramids, just as I was now standing there myself. Names such as Gandhi, Cleopatra, Alexander the Great, Bono, and even distant ancestors of mine. But the most mind-blowing thing was to think of the next generations it would see after I am long gone.

The Sphinx was also much smaller in real life than I had thought it would be, but I guess sometimes that's just the way the human mind works these days: things of great impression must be big in real life. Bigger houses = better; bigger car = better; bigger diamond = better—a byproduct of a capitalist generation, I guess you could say. Bigger is better and better must be bigger.

As I was admiring this great piece of work that has stood the test of time for so long, I paused for a moment and looked in front of me, then I turned around to look back at where I had come from. Ahead of me, standing there as it had done for thousands of years before, was only the oldest Wonder of the Ancient World, the Great Pyramid, and its two sister pyramids—completely alone, surrounded by desert, no water, no trees, just a completely barren landscape. And in the other direction, where the Sphinx was looking, I saw a city of somewhat modern times: big buildings, skyscrapers, and in the foreground, I could even see a KFC and a Pizza Hut. It almost seemed as though the Sphinx was looking forward from the past into the future. It was a true clash of old and new. It was ironic on so many different levels.

As I continued up toward the pyramids, the magnitude of how big they actually were struck me. Of course I had seen bigger modern structures before, wider, larger, taller, but when you stop to realize how these pyramids had been built, it becomes the biggest building you have ever seen. The Great Pyramid stands at 148m high. The stones used to build it weighed anywhere from two to fifty tons. It's in perfect celestial alignment with the constellation Orion. When it was in its full glory, the limestone casing that surrounded it would reflect the sun's rays so much that it could not only be seen from as far away as the mountains in Israel, but also from the moon. And unlike modern buildings, these pyramids were almost virtually solid.

The amount of time and manpower and coordination that must have gone in to building these is astronomical even by today's standards. Moving the stones from anywhere up to 800km away and placing 2.3 million of them into perfect alignment over a twenty-year period. Seems like a lot? Well, get this. That equates to placing one of these gargantuan stones every five minutes, twenty-four hours a day, seven days a week for twenty years.

I remember going inside the Great Pyramid (aka the Pyramid of Khufu). It must have been about 45°C as I climbed down the steep incline, hunched over, as there

162

wasn't enough room to stand. The air became stuffy and the humidity sky-rocketed, which made breathing hard. My shirt was instantly soaking wet from all of the sweat pouring off of me. But at the same time, I was distracted by the surprisingly clear and colorful paintings that had been on the walls for 4,500 years. Eventually, I came to the burial chamber. It was not much bigger than a modern-day living room, but to me, this felt like the heart of the pyramid. This was the reason these mammoth buildings/monuments/shrines/tombs had been built, for the pharaoh's body to lie for eternity in these rooms and so their souls could ascend directly to heaven. It was strange to think that something so small meant so much to one man, who in turn had enough power to make it mean something to so many others for so long during their lives.

/////

After Cairo, I ended up doing a trip along the Nile. Not only is it one of the longest rivers in the world, but it has been a source of life in this region for tens of thousands of years. I stopped at a few places along the way, and one of them that really stood out was Luxor and the Valley of the Kings, situated 7km as the crow flies across the Nile on the west bank.

Luxor (previously known as Thebes) used to be the capital of Egypt, and because of this, it has some of the best remnants of the ancient Egyptian era, including the Karnak Temple Complex, where gargantuan temples dominate the landscape. The temples' size and the effort it must have taken to build them are matched only by that of the pyramids of Giza. Some of the temple columns are 10m tall, and the sandstone they're made of had been brought from 150km away. And there's not just one or two of these massive columns, but tens upon tens of them, maybe even a hundred. Then there's the obelisks of different pharaohs and gods, which stand up to 30m tall and feature artwork and hieroglyphs crafted to such a degree of precision and exquisiteness that they could be mistaken for being made by modern technology, or at least artists and artisans from hundreds and hundreds of years later.

I also saw Deir el-Bahari, which is a another massive temple complex. Instead of being built in the traditional way like other temples in the area, this complex was carved out of a cliff face. It has three layered terraces, each 30m tall. Each layer is articulated by a double colonnade of square piers. These terraces in turn are connected by long, wide ramps running up the middle of the complex, which were once surrounded by lush, colorful gardens—truly an oasis in the desert.

And then came the most well-know Egyptian complex outside of the pyramids of Giza: the Valley of the Kings. It felt so strange, as it gives the impression that you are literally in the middle of nowhere. In fact, except for the highway that took us to that location, I saw nothing else around for as far as I could see—even though it was only 7km from Luxor. It was extremely well hidden amongst the valleys, and even today, it would be quite easily overlooked if it wasn't for the roads leading to it and all the signage. But that was exactly what the ancient Egyptians wanted and why so many of these sites remained hidden for nearly 3,500 years.

As you walk through the actual valley, it looks untouched and unchanged (except for modern developments, clearing bigger paths for tourists, etc.) from what its natural weathered appearance would look like and what you find in any other valley in this region. You walk up the floor of the valley, and as you do, it appears that the way is blocked by natural rock formations running down from the sides of the cliffs. As you approach closer, though, you realize that it is possible to walk around these arms one after the other, alternating from left to right. You end up snaking around the valley in an *S* shape. It's not until you take a closer inspection that you realize that entrances have been built into many of these arms at their bases, where they adjoin the cliffs. Walking around, you would maybe guess from any single point that maybe five or six tombs are spread out around you. In actual fact, they are so well hidden that there are actually over sixty of them. Even modern technology has had trouble detecting them all over the years. The most recent one discovered there was in 2006.

As for the tombs themselves, they are a thousand times more complex than the landscape itself. Creating the burial chambers underground, compared to the inside of a pyramid, meant they weren't limited by space, which ultimately meant that some of them were unbelievably complex—some with over 120 chambers.

Inside is also the best example of ancient Egyptian art, in my opinion—well, definitely the best I've laid eyes upon anyway. Mainly, this is because the artwork is still in its original place and set the way it was intended to be seen, or rather not be seen. Untouched by harmful light for thousands of years, and with most of the tombs being discovered in modern times, it means that there has been no pilfering by thieves or wear and tear from tourism. Although, some of them were discovered not only by tomb robbers but also by tourists up to 2,400 years ago, and you can see by the graffiti and "I was here" inscriptions that people have left over the years.

My next destination where I was to stop and "relax" for a undetermined period of time was a sleepy little place called Dahab on the Red Sea. It has one main strip along the ocean side, filled with cheap hotels and a few bars. I found traditional Bedouin seating out front on the other side of the walkway where I was staying and all along the oceanfront—little square areas laid out next to each other in neat succession, with cushions on the ground for seats, a low table in the middle, and backing with cushions laid against them on three of the sides; the fourth side was open to face the ocean, which lay just meters away. There was no beach at high tide, just water all the way up to the edge. It was shallow water that would start off just toe deep, and for the next 10m gradually get deeper, but only up to your knees. Then, all of a sudden, the ocean floor would drop right out from underneath your feet. A steep descending slope ran away from you until a depth of about 7m . That drop-away was filled with coral and all the interesting marine life that accompanies it.

It was home to some of the most brightly colored fish imaginable, and not just your normal blues, reds, yellows, etc., but electric blues, fiery reds, and fluorescent yellows.

As I explored, the smaller fish that called the reef their home would come to the face of the coral out of curiosity to check you out, and if you startled them, they would be gone just as quickly as they came. Occasionally, a larger fish would venture out, looking for plankton and whatnot to feed off of on the coral. They would cruise along the reef, then all of a sudden at lightning speed, they would snap around and grab a smaller fish or mollusk that had been caught off guard, then swim off into the dark abyss that became the ocean floor farther away from the reef.

Dahab truly is a beautiful place to relax and enjoy water activities—snorkeling along the reef, scuba-diving farther out, sailing, and, from the lounge area every night, you would have a beautiful sunset accompanied by a great view of Saudi Arabia just across the way.

It didn't take me long to meet a fellow traveler whom I got along well with. His name was Raymon and he was from France. Raymon was an accountant and over on a two-week holiday to explore Egypt. We had actually landed in Cairo about the same day and traveled down the Nile at almost the same time, roughly stopping in the same places, and actually arrived in Dahab just one day apart.

166

We had stayed at the same place a couple of times and ended up sitting in the seating area in Dahab right next to each other. Although we'd had so many close encounters, this was the first time we would actually meet each other and strike up some conversation over a couple of beers, some freshly cooked fish caught that morning from the ocean just meters in front of us, and some sheesha. We ended up smoking ourselves stupid that night by trying all the flavors over an eight-hour period and unanimously, drunkenly declaring that "Honey is best" … which we kept repeating and repeating. It would eventually become our random saying: "Ahhh, yes, yes, honey is best."

After a couple days of being lazy and chilling out, we decided to go to Mount Sinai together. We set off by catching a bus that eventually arrived at about three o'clock in the afternoon at our destination. We had planned for this to be somewhat of a solitary journey and to maybe only have a few other people around us along the way, but I'm guessing because of its religious significance, there must have been at least fifty people there. We started near St. Catherine's Monastery, where the bus dropped us off in the car park about 300m away. This was a fascinating place, and to be honest, I knew nothing about it before we arrived. In fact, it remained rather bland to me until we were walking around the grounds and came across a bush that was sitting atop some stone walls that made up a courtyard. It was a massive bush, probably about the size of a small car, and the strange thing was that the vines of the bush overhanging and within reach of the people in the courtyard were stripped of their leaves. This seemed to be a big focal point for the monastery and for a lot of our fellow visitors, so we decided to ask about it. It turned out that this is the very same burning bush from which God spoke to Moses, as recounted in the Bible—the burning bush where an angel appeared to Moses and then Gods' voice told him that he must lead the Jewish people out of Egypt and back to

167

Israel. Just like that, we encountered one of the most important relics from the Old Testament. The surprises of traveling …

After the monastery, we proceeded down a path that led to the foot of Mount Sinai. We could go two ways. First, we could take the aptly named "Camel Path," where camels literally would take less-capable tourists most of the way to the top along a modernish winding road. This journey took about two hours. Or we could go on the much steeper path named the "Penitence Path."

Raymon and I looked at each other and we both knew that we were going to do this the way it was intended to be done: up each and every one of those steps of penitence. We would follow in the footsteps of Moses as he climbed Mount Sinai, once again to hear from God—this time to receive the Ten Commandments.

We started up the 3,750 steps that were hand carved into the mountain by the monks of St. Catherine's Monastery hundreds of years ago. It didn't take long for us to realize just why they were called the steps of penitence. We had no handrails to help, no consideration of the optimum distance between the steps for ease of climbing … just a way to the top. Some of the steps were as small as 10cm and some as big as 50cm. But when you stopped for a breather and looked at where you were, it made it worthwhile. The views back down the valley showed us half of an open, almost Martian landscape of a reddish tint, and the other half massive rock formations carving out valleys as far as the eye could see.

By the time we reached the top, it was getting dark, and unfortunately the sun had already set. But we weren't deterred, because we still had plenty of time until we would witness what we had really come here to see. Our plan was to camp there overnight and then watch the sun rise over the valleys below.

It was a cold and clear night at the top, and we

probably would have frozen to death if it wasn't for the sleeping bags we'd brought. We didn't have much shelter up there, except for a small chapel (literally about two meters by two meters) that had been built about a hundred years ago on top of previous ruins, a building method that had been the tradition for hundreds of years. The chapel itself was locked, but the walls still made a good windbreak. No fires were allowed on the top of the mountain, not that there was any wood around to burn anyway. Still, if you brought your own little burner and the fire got out of control, I could understand how devastated the monks would be and how it would affect tourism.

As for the flashlights we had brought with us, we never needed to use them, because our night was lit by the brightest of bright moons. You could see it lighting various parts of the valleys below, cutting its path through like a silvery scarf that had floated to the ground from the heavens above. And being that no cities were around, nothing tainted the brightness of the billions of stars on the other side of the sky. Together, it looked like a frozen moment or photograph of a light, silvery snowfall that was somehow only falling on one swath on the land, which was winding its way over the landscape.

We awoke to our alarms at about 5:00 a.m. The clear and crisp night led to a chilly morning. It was so cold and we were so snug that we didn't want to get out of our sleeping bags. So we just propped ourselves up against a couple of boulders on the far side of the open top of the mountain so as to get the best view. We were both still tired and neither of us were morning people, so there wasn't much conversation going on at that moment in time.

There was an intense silence all around. There were no birds to sing their early morning songs and no modern city noise to break through the static of the silence. There was no wind blowing, and no wildlife anywhere to be seen. It was just literally deathly still silence, to a degree that I

169

had never before been exposed to. We couldn't even hear the slight residual ringing of the world around us in our ears, which is normally present during silence.

Before too long, the horizon was broken by the first rays of light of the new day. It was like the sky was divided directly into two opposing pieces, yin and yang, heaven and earth.

At one end, you still had the moon shining brightly, creating a white halo arcing across the horizon, coming closer and closer to setting behind the distant, still darkened mountains. Then directly above it, hundreds of stars still hovered ever so faintly in the dying night sky, slowly being extinguished by the ever more forthcoming light.

And on the other side, the true master of the sky, the sun, slowly painting its colors of faint yellow and red onto the dull gray-blue sky, creating a work of art that would be our new day.

We watched this fleeting moment in complete silence as the night was slowly engulfed by the new day, almost unaware of each other's presence until finally, unfortunately, all to soon it was over and we were released from its mesmerizing display of beauty and tranquility.

I could see why a man would believe that God was talking to him in this place.

A few hours later, we returned to where we were staying in Dahab. It was late morning by the time we got back, and we hadn't had anything to eat since the afternoon before. We decided to go straight to the shore where we usually ate, but we couldn't find any free lounges available. We decided to ask if we could join a couple of guys that were in our usual spot.

"Of course, please, we would love you to," they said.

They turned out to be two Israelis. One was a native of Russia (Sergei) who had served five years with the Israeli army to gain his citizenship. And the other (Nadav) was Israeli born, but just for the record, he also had to serve three years with the Israeli army because every citizen has to; even the women must serve two years.

It was interesting to have a conversation with people that had grown up in a society where this sort of thing was the norm: bluntly put, a place where, once everyone comes of age, the very first thing that society does to them is train them to kill other human beings. Of course, I knew there was many more aspects to life as an Israeli living in Israel, and I never put my own thoughts so directly to them. It was just the way my mind bluntly pondered these blatant differences, which really struck my curiosity. It made me more and more interested in learning about the culture and spending time with the people.

*One day, I will definitely go there,* I thought.

But that opportunity of "one day" came sooner than I thought. After speaking to Nadav and Sergei for about another hour, I received an invite to go to Israel.

"If you want, you can come and stay with me in Haifa, and Nadav and I will show you around," Sergei said.

I looked over at Raymon and gave him a look as if to say, "What do you think?"

After all, I had only just met these guys a couple of hours ago.

"Why not?" Raymon said as he shrugged his shoulders to emphasize that he couldn't think of a reason why I shouldn't.

I wasn't going to let this opportunity slip by. *Carpe diem. Time to take a little risk and make this adventure even more memorable.* Two days later, I was off to Israel.

# CHAPTER 16

## *SHALOM*

I found it daunting to go through a border like the one between Taba in Egypt and Eilat in Israel. The security is extraordinarily tight, and all the customs officers (carrying sidearms at the least if not semiautomatic machine guns) had looks on their faces like everyone was out to get them and everyone was a suspect—even a twenty-one-year-old kid just traveling to see the world. But I had my new friends with me, and I was more than glad because the customs officials didn't speak a word of English. Well, they more than likely did, but I think it was more of a case that they didn't want to. You could tell they were young cocky bastards who didn't want anyone entering their country who didn't have a birth/heritage rite to be there. I had to go through a different channel than Nadav and Sergei due to the fact that I wasn't a resident. Almost as soon as I came to the immigration officer, I ran into trouble. But luckily, Nadav and Sergei saw me struggling and came to my rescue. They had a little argument with the guy who was hassling me, but I didn't know what they were saying. They later told me, "He was just being an ass because he can and has the power to, like a lot of people around in this country."

On the other side of the border, we would go our separate ways. Although I had decided to come to Israel and stay with my friends up in the north, I was never going to go straight past the ancient city of Jerusalem. I would have never been able to forgive myself for letting my fears get in my way of visiting a place such as that.

Nadav almost immediately hopped on to a bus and was off to his home town of Haifa. Sergei, though, was

172

going to visit a friend and had to catch a different bus, coincidently the same one I had to catch to get to Jerusalem. Although, I had the feeling that he didn't have to catch that bus; he just pretended he had to because I think he could see in my eyes that I was a little intimidated about where I was. That bus did end up in Haifa as well; it just took an extra four hours to arrive there.

I remember when I first got off of the bus from Eilat. I wasn't sure where I was going and had no idea of a place to stay. It was about 5:00 a.m. in the morning, and everywhere in the old town was closed. It didn't look very hospitable, either, with barred windows and doors everywhere. As I was wandering around looking for a place to stay, I came across the old wall of the Temple Mount, also known as the Wailing Wall—which was in fact the only remaining wall of the Second Temple that was built on the site after the first was destroyed.

The Wailing Wall is the second-most holy place in Judaism and the closet place that the Jews are allowed to the Temple Mount, or the Dome of the Rock as it is better known, which is said to be the holiest place on earth. The reason why they aren't allowed any closer is because the Dome of the Rock is "owned" by the Muslims. It is believed that a prayer at the Wailing Wall will go directly to heaven and God himself. This is reinforced by the fact that you see tens of thousands of little pieces of paper with prayers written on them, all stuffed into the cracks in the wall, left by hundreds of thousands of people.

The Dome of the Rock, which is directly behind the Wailing Wall, is a temple, and its foundation stone located in the center is believed to be the spot where the prophet Mohammed ascended to heaven with the archangel Gabriel. It is also traditionally considered the place where the Holy of Holies stood, with the Ark of the Covenant that contained the tablets of the Ten Commandments, which Moses received on top of Mount Sinai directly from God, as we saw a bit ago. It is also believed to be the place where Abraham prepared to sacrifice his son Isaac to God. For many years, this place was known as the most holy spot on earth for three of the world's major religions: Christianity, Judaism, and Islam. The Jews still do pray toward it, and originally the Muslims did as well, until it was changed to Mecca because of an argument Mohammed had with a Jewish tribe.

Looking down upon the wall from a staircase, I decided I wanted to go and have a look. On my way walking down, a young man came up to me and greeted me. He asked where I was from and what I was doing there. I explained to him how I had always wanted to come and see Jerusalem, and his eyes lit up. It seemed that he presumed that I was Jewish (I think because, in his mind, he thought why would anyone want to come and see such historical sites unless they were deeply religious). Rather than disappoint him and ruin his conversation, I played along with him and told him I was half-Jewish. His eyes lit up even further and he proceeded to tell me that I must see and pray at the wall immediately. At the time, I didn't realize that "photo" tourists weren't allowed up to the wall, as it was reserved for the religious prayers. So, by my luck, he took me through the gates and past the ever-present security guards, telling them that I was Jewish and on a pilgrimage. So, with my backpack on, I proceeded to go up to the Wailing Wall to check it out for myself.

As high as a person could reach, in every nook and cranny in the wall, I saw little crumpled-up notes on which people had written their messages to God. This was surely one of the holiest of holy places for the Jewish people, the closest place on earth to the throne of God. And, as tradition goes, when the Jews pray from all over the world, they pray toward this wall, and their prayers ascend to God directly from here, virtually the same as what the Kaaba in Mecca is to the Muslims.

My newfound friend came up to me and gave me a prayer book and a kippah to wear (the small little skullcap the Jews wear when praying and even sometimes in everyday life). In return, I gave him my camera and told him it would make my family very happy if he could take a photo. Before I knew it, I was facing the wall pretending to say my prayers. I had no idea what I was doing and just played along. Everyone else was rocking back and forth while they were praying, so I thought I would do the same. Everyone was also reading a passage from their prayer book, so I opened mine up, picked a random page, and began to read. It was an incredibly exhilarating experience. To feed off of the energy that people were aiming toward that wall gave me a buzz. Maybe it was also the thrill of pretending to do something people presumed I had done many times before.

After I got my photo and had my moment of "glory" at the wall, I decided to ask my new friend if he knew of a hostel where I could stay in the city. His eyes instantly lit up as he proclaimed he knew of one.

"They don't charge for accommodations, either," he said—with a little too much enthusiasm for my liking.

As we were walking to the place, I asked him why it was free, as well as a bunch of other questions, including how he knew the place, and did he have anything to do with it directly or indirectly. But he always managed to tiptoe around the questions and avoided giving me a straight answer, just like everyone's favorite politician would. This tended to be the norm around these parts, either that or answering with a riddle or a parable. Everyone thought they were wiser than the last person here and subsequently had their own lesson to pass on.

For example:

"How can a place afford to stay open when it is not charging?" I asked.

"Because by people coming here, they educate their

175

souls, and when other people educate their souls, money comes from others who see it as enlightening the world and a worthwhile investment," he replied.

Or when I asked him, "Why are you helping me so much?"

"Well, one day, there was a village that was being terrorized by a lion. The people were struck with fear and afraid to go outside. The lion would roam around looking for food and be aggressive to anyone it saw. All the people were terrified of it. Until one day, a brave young boy came along and went up to the lion as it roared and snarled at him with all its might, but he stood his ground right in front its face, showing no fear. When he was just inches from its jaws, he noticed that the lion had a thorn in its foot. Immediately, the boy pulled the thorn out and the lion groaned with relief. The lion was so grateful and relieved that it left the people, and they once again went about their business and didn't have to live in fear."

"Uh-huh," I said in a manner that I hoped would tell him I wasn't impressed by his parable. *What a long, drawn-out, indirect, time-wasting, stupid way to answer a question as straightforward as mine,* I thought.

Before I even had a chance to breathe, I realized that the eye contact I'd kept with him throughout his story out of respect was actually being taken as me showing an interest. So he started telling another story, hoping that he could inspire and enlighten me further. I stopped him soon after he started, and said, "Oh, yes, I understand," so as to avoid the rest of his next analogy. But it didn't work. Somehow he still got the impression I wanted to hear the rest of the story.

When we finally arrived at the place, it looked like any other hostel. It was located down a poorly lit alley, but that tended to be like most of the stone streets, alleys, and lanes in the Old City. The place was like a maze, and there were no vehicles around because the streets were so

176

narrow. The difference between day and night was literally day and night. There would be people selling all sorts of things on the street sides during the day, people bustling around, all the usual sights and sounds that you would expect of a city. But at nighttime, the place was deserted and the security was tight, massive locks on doors and barred windows everywhere you turned.

There was no answer at the door when we first rang and knocked, as even the accommodation places were closed overnight. Luckily, though, my new acquaintance had the guy's phone number and decided to give him a call. I couldn't imagine I would have had to wait there too long anyway, because by now the sun was up, people had been stirring for a while, and businesses were starting to open. Someone finally came to let us in after about ten minutes, and I proceeded to the front desk. I was greeted by a young man with a beard, skullcap, and the traditional payot hair (the long curls of hair that hang down over the ears of some Orthodox Jews due to the thought that the Torah directs against the shaving of the side of one's head and beard, apparently originally started to stop the offering of one's hair to the dead, thought to protect the soul in the underworld).

The first thing he said to me even before "Hello" was to politely ask me how long I wanted to stay.

"I'm not too sure," I said, and before I could throw in "Maybe three to four days," he jumped in and said, "As long as you need a home, this home will suit your needs."

*Right,* I thought. "So a few days, if that is okay?" I said.

"Yes, of course," the man replied with a smile.

Then he immediately struck up a conversation in Hebrew with my friend. By the body language, I deduced that it was about me.

"Come," the man said, "put your things in your room and I will show you around."

"Thanks," I replied.

With that, my new friend was off, saying only, "I will see you soon when we enlighten our minds together once again."

I smiled and nodded.

I put my things into my room and proceeded to get the tour of a place.

"Here is the kitchen, here is the living room, and here is the study," the man said.

"The study?" I asked.

"Yes, so people can study when they get back at night in peace and quiet, or the library, which is the next door along."

*Interesting,* I thought, but said nothing, not wanting to ask too many questions.

"Anyway," he said, "we have an information session every day at 2:00 p.m. you should come to."

I presumed the sessions were about the city, so I didn't ask any questions about it. "Oh, great," I said. "I don't really want to wait around for eight hours, though. I want to get out and see more of the city today, so how about tomorrow?"

"Ah, yes, I love your enthusiasm to immerse yourself in the biblical surroundings you are in. You will fit in very well here when it comes time for lessons."

As I looked into his eyes, he gave me the look and body language that implied he had just let a little secret slip.

"Yeah, right," I said.

I didn't think too much of it and wasn't interested in any game he was going to try and play, as I thought he was just talking about the everyday lessons that we all stumble across. So, with that, I was off to explore the city.

I first went and saw the Church of the Holy Sepulchre, which is a church that was built to surround and somewhat house the area where Jesus had been crucified on the cross, where his body was prepared for burial, and the cave into which he was placed and arose from the dead three days later. The stone slab on which Jesus's body was thought to have been laid out is the centerpiece in my opinion. It has its own little room in the church, and you have to hunch over to go inside. Once you are in, it is literally a stone slab, maybe six feet by three feet, and about the same amount of floor space beside it.

I then visited the grave of Oskar Schindler—one of the most famous members of the German Nazi Party during World War II. Schindler was a originally tradesman, and a few years before the war, he joined the German intelligence service, then in 1936 joined the Nazi Party and served as a spy for them in Poland. He played a small role in facilitating the invasion of Poland by the Nazis. After spending time in jail in Czechoslovakia for espionage charges, and running into trouble in Poland as well, he decided for a career change. He purchased an enamel factory in Poland and, with his past military contacts, landed a contract to produce goods for the German military. This in turn made his factory a lucrative business, and he made a lot of money.

He originally hired a number of Jews for the simple fact that they were cheaper to pay than Poles (this was determined by the Nazis). As the war unfolded, though, and the truth about the atrocities committed by the Nazis came out, Schindler took on more and more Jews to save them and their families from deportation and extermination. Because his factory was deemed essential toward the Nazi war effort, the Germans spared every Jew working at the factory, along with their families. Schindler's efforts, then, took a large shift from making money to saving lives. He fed them, clothed them, built a camp for some of them, paid bribes to keep suspicious SS officers from causing issues, and by the end of the war, had saved an estimated 1,200 lives.

"I hated the brutality, the sadism, and the insanity of Nazism. I just couldn't stand by and see people destroyed. I did what I could, what I had to do, what my conscience told me I must do. That's all there is to it. Really, nothing more," Oskar Schindler said later.

I also visited the Church of the Sepulchre of Saint Mary at the foot of the Mount of Olives, where it is believed the Virgin Mary is buried—or was buried until she ascended to heaven body and all, depending on what teachings, if any, you believe.

After having some baba ghanoush (like I did in Turkey) for dinner, I headed back to my hostel to get an early night. Standing in the alleyway in front of the place while ringing the buzzer, I thought, *I don't remember this place being so imposing.* In front of me was a big iron-barred gate instead of a door that you had to get buzzed into. Iron bars barricaded all of the windows, which were hid behind shutters. Plus, they had security cameras pointing straight at your face. All of this felt even more imposing because of a couple of Israeli soldiers in full gear walking past with their machine guns. Finally, the door buzzed, so I pushed it open and hurried in off the street. When I got to my shared dorm room, I saw another guy there. I remember him very clearly. He was sitting on the top bunk in the corner of the room, and I could tell he had noticed me come into the room and was watching me as discreetly as possible.

"Hey, how are you?" I asked.

"Yes, fine, thank you," he said in his American accent.

"Where are you from?"

"The S-S-St-States."

He sounded nervous and had a skittish sense about him. He wasn't making eye contact and was fiddling with a backpack that he had between his legs on his bed. I decided to try a little bit more conversation to try and loosen him up a bit.

"Why are you here? Traveling?" I asked.

"No, I am studying here."

"Studying what?"

"The Torah [the Jewish holy book]. I used to travel, but now I study here. Now I am here. This is what I do. I was, like you, a traveler."

I was thrown a bit by how he fumbled his sentences around.

"Soooo you did a bit of traveling, then decided to come here to study?"

He shook his head. "No, I never intended to stay here. I just wanted to travel, but I never had the money, so my parents paid for it but told me I had to come here to stay when I was in Jerusalem for a couple of weeks, so I agreed." He rushed through the sentence as if he had practiced it a thousand times before.

"So why are you still here?"

"Well, I don't know. I came here and was talking to the owners, and the things they say, it made a lot sense to me. You know, in terms of life and direction."

"So you like studying the Torah?"

Another shake of his head. "No, I am not religious."

"But you're studying the Bible of the Jews."

"Yes, I know," he said as he twitched slightly and closed off his body language a little more toward me.

"Do you actually want to be here?"

"No, I hate it, but this is where God wants me to be."

"But you're not religious."

"Yes, I know."

And with that, he'd had enough of my prying, jumped off of his bed, donned his kippah, said he had to go study, and was out of there.

*Wow,* I thought. *This must be their game, to sucker people here [even though he had been pushed into it by his*

*parents, but I hadn't] and recruit them to study the Torah,*
*brainwash them, and then who knows what. After all, they*
*did think I was Jewish.*

So the next day, I awoke, bright and early, got my
things, and was out of there. The guy at reception tried to
convince me to stay.

"You can stay. It is fine. You don't have to study if
you don't want to," he said without me even implying that
was the problem.

I knew, though, that the longer I stayed, the more
they would slowly pressure and guilt me into taking their
"lessons," and then who knows what slowly over time.

"No, that's not it," I said. "I've decided to go and
see the Dead Sea."

"Well, I can take you," he said, and I presumed it
was so he could keep me in the circle a little bit longer.

"No, that's fine. I have arrangements, thank you,
but I will be back here in a couple of weeks," I said, just to
stop him from pressuring me. "Thanks and see you soon."

"Fantastic. I look forward to it," he said as his body
manner changed from sad to overexcited—way too excited
for the situation.

And with that, I was out of there. I wandered around
and in no time found another place to stay, and once again
spent my days exploring more of the Old City. There are so
many interesting things to see around the Old City of
Jerusalem. I would in fact have to go as far as to say it is
the most, if not second-most, interesting city I have been to.
Yes, there are better individual things in many other places,
but in terms of so many things in one place, it's hard to
beat. Then, you throw that together with the extremes in
multiculturalism, history, and religion in an area that is
divided up into five quarters—yes, five: Christian, Muslim,
Jewish, Armenian, and the unofficial Afro-Palestinian
quarter. Add all that up, and it just makes the place reek of
adventure and culture. And true to what its surroundings

182

imply, this was where my real Israeli adventure would start.

# CHAPTER 17

## ALI JIDDAH: PATRIOT OR TERRORIST?

The Old City of Jerusalem has a history five thousand years old. It has not only been the adopted epicenter and crossroads between the continents of Africa, Asia, and Europe for millennia, but it also has been ruled by great empires such as the Babylonians, Persians, Greeks, Romans, and Byzantines. It was even made its own kingdom by the European Crusaders, and ruled by various other empires right through to the Ottoman and British empires before it was made an independent country. It's also one of the main epicenters for close to 60 percent of the world's religious followers. And even though it's an area of only 900m squared, it has a population of 35,000, meaning that if it was considered a city itself, it would be one of the most densely populated in the world.

This old section of Jerusalem is also a breeding ground for the most interesting characters. Angels, pilgrims, beggars, merchants, students of great scholars, warriors, and slaves have all walked its streets. The Old City of Jerusalem is without a doubt the most historically interesting city I have ever visited, even to this day. This chapter, then, focuses on just one of the many individuals that I met there. He turned out to be one of the most interesting men, and he would provide me with one of my most interesting experiences in all of my years of traveling the world.

I was up early in the morning as usual, trying to get in the most exploration I could out of my days in the Old City of Jerusalem. Surprisingly, I didn't see that many people around. I put it down to the fact that most people who lived in the Old City probably worked in the new city, the modern Jerusalem with its airport, train, and bus networks, and skyscrapers.

I remained wary while wandering around the city, thinking about my safety after all the stories I had heard and read about, of bombs going off and buses being blown up. After my experiences there, though, I now look back and think how naïve and paranoid I was, and I've come to realize that Israel for the most part is a safe place to travel around. The people have a certain amount of respect for each other, and it seems to be a slightly more disciplined society than a lot of others I have traveled through. When we hear through the media that Israel suffered another terrorist attack and innocent people died, we think that this is an everyday occurrence, but it is not. In fact, per capita, Israel has roughly the same homicide rate as Australia, with the main difference being that street crime in Israel is virtually nonexistent. Homicides are mostly related to honor killings and terrorism, so in my opinion, you have more to worry about walking around the streets at night in Australia than Israel.

So I went exploring the narrow walkways and pathways, not paying too much attention to my map, as I just wanted to see what I came across. In the unofficial Afro-Palestinian quarter of the Old City, I found a small shop with a group of men sitting out the front, drinking tea and smoking sheesha. It was still fairly early in the morning, and there weren't many people around. As I walked by, one of them stopped me and initiated a conversation. Just the usual "How are you? Where are you from? What are you doing here?" But I ended up sitting there for about two hours having a few rather in-depth and interesting conversations.

One of the men, named Ali, told me he had some business he had to do and asked if I would like to join him so that he could also show me around a few of the sites outside of the Old City. I wholeheartedly agreed, even

185

though I was not sure where we were going. So we hopped in his car and started talking about the Israeli/Palestinian situation, and as an outsider, I shared my knowledge of its publicity in the media overseas. I proceeded to tell him my honest opinion about how his people are mostly portrayed in Western media as the villains, but I also made sure I added that I thought this was obviously a biased opinion put forth by the Israelis and how more than a few people thought that way. I told him I had never met a Palestinian before.

To which, he asked, "Are you not afraid?"

"No," I replied. "I like to consider myself a good judge of character, and I realize people can only be judged by the society they are brought up in to a certain extent, and to me, it seems like you have a good heart."

We got along well, and he grew ever more enthusiastic about showing me around, not just the new Jerusalem but also Palestine, so I could learn and see for myself. He was curious to hear more about my own formed opinions, as he thought they showed wisdom beyond my years.

"My friend, tomorrow once again you should come with me," he said. "I will take you to the West Bank to see the sites. It would be my pleasure."

The borders between Israel and Palestine were hard to navigate in the best of times: only open for certain hours of the day, if at all; sometimes closed to nonresidents; and having no real public transportation there, let alone on the other side to carry on through the West Bank.

*Wow, I can't pass up such a great opportunity like this.* So I told him that I'd be happy to go with him.

I'd thought that I might have to miss out on seeing places like Bethlehem because of the logistics and ever-changing rules and regulations at the border crossings. And I couldn't afford to have some luxury tour company full of rich religious tourists from half a world away take me.

186

*What a fantastic opportunity,* I thought ... and at the same time, I clenched my fists, wondering what I might be getting myself into.

So I awoke early next morning and met Ali at the coffee shop we had agreed to meet at. I walked in, and with the shop being not busy yet, I spotted him straightaway. Ali is a tall man, at about six-two, with dark skin (being an Afro-Palestinian), a completely bald head, and a thin build with a tiny belly. I guessed him to be in his early fifties. Ali was sitting at a table by himself, leaning back in his chair and drinking an espresso coffee, his legs crossed at the thighs. He had red reading glasses perched on the end of his nose, giving him the look of man who was intrigued by the newspaper he was indulging in at the time. I walked over to him and said, "Hello." He was briefly silent while he finished reading something, then he looked up and a big smile engulfed his face.

"Ah, Adam, my friend! I am glad you decided to come."

"Ali, yes, thank you. Nice to see you again. Of course, I wouldn't miss this for the world."

"Ah, yes. You are too kind. I like your enthusiasm. You are an open-minded and curious young man. Israel needs more people like you here. Now, should we get going?"

"Ready whenever you are."

After a brief conversation with the man behind the counter, who appeared to be Ali's friend, we were off.

About an hour later, we arrived at the armistice line, which was a politically correct way of saying "border," given the heated international politics behind the Israel/Palestine situation. We arrived at the checkpoint and parked, since it was nearly impossible to cross the border with a vehicle. We saw a few other tourists trying to get in, but they were turned away by the Israelis.

"Come this way," Ali said. "Come this way. I know

187

a man."

So we proceeded to walk to the far side of the checkpoint, where locals were moving in and out. Ali had what seemed to be a friendly conversation with one of the Palestinian guards that he knew. The guard looked me up and down, smiled, and then handed us what would later turn out to be a couple of fake media IDs. We then walked back to where the Israelis were controlling the entrance and lined up with all of the other Palestinians who just wanted to get across the border, probably to their homes and families, or returning from doing some shopping or visiting friends in that district. The border, though, was controlled by Israelis who seemed to go out of their way to make it a slow and painful process, seemingly out of spite.

I don't know why, but I wasn't nervous standing there in the line. I almost felt privileged and a little bit thrilled while looking at all of the other tourist getting turned away, some of whom presumably had come from half a world away just to see these religious places of interest but were getting denied passage nonetheless.

As we approached the guards, I caught the attention of one of them. He walked up to me with a smile on his face and said something to me in Hebrew, which I obviously didn't understand. I smiled politely and asked him if he spoke English, as I knew it was very common for younger, under-thirty Israelis to speak English. I would almost go as far to say that it is the second language in the country, with Russian and Arabic following closely behind.

"You are not Israeli?" he asked in English.

"No."

"Well, this border is closed to tourists today. Sorry, brother," he said. "Come back next week if you have to, but I wouldn't bother at all if I were you."

Before the disappointment had a chance to sink in or I could even respond, Ali grabbed my passport from my hand and, along with the two IDs, forcefully pushed them

188

toward the guard.

"Here you go," Ali said. "We are here for business. How rash you are to presume that we are too stupid to see that borders are closed to tourists today, and just coincidently lined up in the non-tourist line. Does it look like we are brothers coming for a holiday? No, we are journalists doing a story. Now, if you wouldn't mind ..."

My smile had sunk from my face and became a look of surprised disapproval at the tone of voice and bluntness Ali used with the border guard. I could tell from the manner in his voice that he intended to be polite, but he also didn't want to give the impression that he was the kind of person who could just be walked all over. I wasn't sure if the guard would take it the same way, though.

A pause, and the guard finally said, "Yes, yes. Okay, you can go straight through."

With that, Ali puffed up his chest and told me to come along, and we walked through the border crossing.

By the end of my time in Israel, I would come to see that the Israelis were a blunt and direct people. They always seemed to have a seriousness about them, even when laughing over a few drinks. They also tended to have a look of experience in their eyes, like they had all seen the harsh realities of living in this region of the world. This could likely be credited to the fact that, besides living in an unstable region where the threat of violence always existed, they all had served in the military.

On the other side of the border, Ali and I walked a few blocks until we were at some kind of unmarked taxi rank. As he always seemed to, Ali knew one of the men and negotiated for him to drive us around for the whole day for US$20 and lunch—a bargain anyplace in the world. So, with the finer details out of the way, we were off.

During the course of our conversations and exploration, I would ask Ali where specifically we were going to next. But he liked to keep an air of mystery about

189

it for some reason and would just reply with something along the lines of "Oh, don't worry, my friend. We are going somewhere interesting. You will be impressed. We are almost there." I didn't mind Ali playing coy to my questions, though. It gave the journey a sense of more adventure, and I looked forward to each surprise.

At one point, we arrived in a small city to the south of Jerusalem, with me having no idea at all where we were. Ali ushered me out of the car and we hurried down a few back roads. We walked around a corner and came into in a courtyard of some sort where the pavement had been virtually destroyed. At the far side of the small courtyard stood two adjoining walls of a very old building. As I stood there, Ali pointed out all of the bullet holes that had burrowed their way into the cement of the ancient relic. He said the holes came from a siege that had happened there barely a year ago. It lasted for thirty-nine days and claimed eight lives. It turned out that the pavement was a shambles because the Israelis had driven their tanks through and the sheer weight had caused it be crushed like fresh snow under a human foot. We were at the Church of the Nativity, in Bethlehem.

The ever-mysterious Ali told me that he had a couple of things to do and was going to visit a friend around the corner. He said he would meet me back there in either an hour or whenever I was ready. I had actually wanted to explore by myself a bit, because I knew I would be able to appreciate where I was a lot more if I was alone.

So, after Ali went his way, I approached the entrance of the church. One monk sat at the small doorway, which was barely at my shoulder height and seemed like an unusual entrance for the millions of people that had passed through here before me. I said "Hello" to the monk and he gave me a polite smile. He almost had a look of bewilderment on his face. Was it because maybe he thought I was Israeli and wondered why I was there? Or was it because I looked too young to be there alone? Or did I still have some breakfast on my face? He went on to tell me that normally there would be a lineup of pilgrims for hours on end, all trying to get in to see this holy place. But, because the Israelis had closed the border, I was the first non-Palestinian that they had seen in six months. As soon as these words left his lips, my thoughts immediately shifted toward my safety.

"Huh. Wow," I replied.

He must have noticed the slight look of concern on my face. "But don't worry," he said. "You have nothing to fear here. They closed the border to keep us out of there, not the other way around." He smiled. "Please go in. I will show you, if you like."

So I hunched my back, stepped through the doorway, and soon was on a personal guided tour of the Church of the Nativity—the church that had been built over the cave where Jesus Christ was said to have been born.

Entering the church, what immediately struck me were the four rows of eleven massive white-veined, red-stone pillars, which stood maybe three or four times my height and ran the length of the church. They were all decorated with a fantastic range of artwork depicting everything from Knights Templar and wildlife to scenes of importance throughout Christian history. One of the most interesting was a face of Jesus that created the optical illusion of his eyes sometimes being open and sometimes being shut.

Moving forward, I noticed a section of the floor that had been removed to reveal mosaics that were hundreds of years old, all of which belonged to the floor of the original chapel that had been built. The detail and color were still preserved. Walking farther down, my newfound friend pointed out some strange-looking holes in one of the pillars. They were in the shape of a cross and about as deep as the thickness of a finger—which was exactly how they

191

had been made. People who've come here over the millennia first traced their fingers on the column in the shape of a cross as they prayed to God. Over the years, the depressions have become deeper and deeper through being worn down by the touch of so many fingers.

Also, strangely, this part of the column was magnetic—strange because the columns are made from limestone, a non-magnetic stone. I wouldn't have believed it if the monk hadn't pulled out a local coin and stuck it there.

Toward the back of the church stood an altar, and to each side was a small staircase that led downward into what they call the grotto. We walked down the steps, and after one turn, I found myself in an underground room about twelve meters long and four wide. The man simply said to me, "Over there, where those four oil lamps are, is where the four wise men stood as they presented gifts to the baby Jesus. And there in that very spot, marked by that silver star on the floor surrounded by the white marble well in the very center, is where our Lord and Savior Jesus Christ entered this world. Now I will leave you alone," he said.

"Can you take a picture of me, please, before you leave?" I asked.

"Oh, yes, of course."

He took my camera, then snapped a picture of me as I bent down and touched the spot where Jesus Christ was said to have been born. And then the monk was off up the stairs.

I am not an overly religious person, but it was definitely an awe-inspiring experience. To be alone there, touching the very spot, walking around the very place where Western society's main religion had been created over two thousand years ago ... where so many people before had come from the other side of the world to pray at this very spot ... where they would have had to wait for sometimes hours and hours in a line, then only have a few seconds because of the crowds before they were ushered on.

As for myself, I had the luxury and intimacy of all the time in the world.

I stood on the spot where so many millions of people from all around the world believed the age of enlightenment had begun ... the place where the dawn of the teachings of tolerance and forgiveness had started ... the place where their Savior had come to change the world forever.

It doesn't matter if you are religious or not, if you have any interest in humanity whatsoever, you have to be in awe of this place—being such a center of focus and hope for so many people from so many countries and from so many different walks of life.

After I met back up with Ali, we stopped in Jericho, one of the oldest inhabited cities in the world, with artifacts and evidence of civilization dating back twelve thousand years. It is also the place where the fabled impenetrable walls of Jericho had crumbled to the ground, brought down by a single blow of a horn. It's also where Jesus performed one of his many miracles.

But by far, the most interesting nonreligious place he took me to was Ramallah, his hometown and the capital of Palestine.

One of the first places Ali showed me was Yasser Arafat's palace, or compound, where he was holed up and had been for years. Half the buildings had been destroyed by bombs and artillery. I could see into rooms and plainly see the objects within: chairs, tables, and even a bed in one. It was like someone had made a cross section of the building, with the waste just strewn all about on the ground below. Mountains of rubble lay here and there, having not been touched for months. Never before had I seen or did I think I would ever see so much destruction in such a densely populated area. I couldn't believe that this was happening in a country that claimed to be so Western and modern, as Israel did. It made me think more about how a situation like this could arise and why there were no sanctions on Israel, as would happen to any other country in the world, where so many organizations would deem it an occupying force and label it an insult to international law.

We walked down one of the main streets of downtown Ramallah, where major political rallies, demonstrations, and massacres had happened. It seemed like Ali knew everyone. Many people, young and old, would go out of their way to come and talk to him, to just say hello or to shake his hand. For some reason, he seemed to be a celebrity. I certainly was introduced to a lot of wonderful and interesting people—and got more than my fair share of strange looks.

As we kept on walking, Ali asked me how I felt.

"In terms of what?" I said.

"Do you feel comfortable walking around?"

"Yes, fairly. Why? Is there something I should be a bit more concerned about?"

He laughed. "My friend, the only reason you haven't been shot yet is because you are with me."

*Oh Christ!* I thought, then asked, "What do you mean?"

"My friend, you are in Palestine. No man here has a problem with Australians, but to them, you look like an Israeli. There is no difference between your look. Ha-ha-ha."

I had a feeling that he was playing up the situation a bit, just to put things in perspective a little more for me. But one thing did feel 100 percent certain to me. Although extremism was rarely seen there, it definitely did exist, maybe in one out of a hundred people. And I had no doubt that if I stayed there long enough, eventually I would come across someone who would mistake me for an Israeli and do something about it.

But, being a naïve twenty-one-year-old at the time, this thought had never really crossed my mind until then.

"Never fear," Ali said. "You are with me. You will be more than safe. But, for now, it is time to go. Come with me. If you like, I will show you my home. Or if you would like to go back, we need to leave now, because after 5:00, you cannot cross the border until morning again."

I must admit, at that time, the thought of this seemed a bit scary, but as I pondered more in depth about it, that itch once again began on my arm—the one that would come to remind me periodically of why I got *Carpe Diem* tattooed there. To do exactly that: seize the moment. When else would I have an opportunity like this, to stay in the capital of Palestine with one of the locals? So off we went to his house just outside of the city, and along the way we picked up a few of his friends, some beer, and some fresh meat. At his house, we enjoyed a lovely food called "mansaf," which is a traditional Bedouin meal from the region. It is a relatively lavish meal compared to what they normally eat, due to the complexities of getting anything but the food essentials in the region. Therefore, it is reserved for special occasions. I was feeling lucky and honored that they considered this a special occasion and was more than happy to pay the $7 that everything cost as a gesture of kindness, but it was refused. I also came to the conclusion that some of Ali's errand running had been to acquire some of the harder-to-get ingredients in anticipation of our special meal. I'm sure he had to pull a few strings to get some of them. .

Mansaf is a leg of lamb on top of taboon bread, which is a flat bread that can be opened up so it is like a pocket that can be filled. Then the meat is smothered with yellow rice. A type of thick, dried cheese yogurt from goat's milk (called jameed) is then poured on top of the lamb and rice to give the dish its distinct flavor. Finally, the

195

whole thing is garnished with almonds, pine nuts, onions, and tomatoes.

It had a sourly tangy taste to it because of the natural yogurt, but turned out to be a tasty meal. I was shocked at first when Ali ripped a chunk of meat off the bone with his hands and handed it to me. But I soon noticed that everyone was ripping meat with their right hand and passing it to someone else to then eat with the taboon bread. I learned that it was a tradition and a politeness that accompanied this meal, to share it with your friends. So I dove right in, ripped a chunk of flesh from the leg, then smiled at the guy across from me as he smiled back. I extended my hand and he received it while saying "Thank you" and touching his chest with his other hand, along with a slight bow of his head with sincerity.

And with that, we proceeded to drink beer and talk about politics, religion, and life in general into the night.

# CHAPTER 18

## LOVE THY NEIGHBOR

Five of us stayed at Ali's house that night. Well, I say five, but there were two more, actually. I wasn't sure who the others were, but I presumed they were female partners or relatives of the other men at the house. In fact, I wasn't even sure it was actually Ali's house, as apparently it was common for them to call a friend's house their own house as well. It was meant to imply that it the house was always open and welcome to you or your friends. At the same time, it was and still is quite common in Muslim culture for women to remain in the background. The traditional roles of looking after children and doing the cooking, etc., were clearly implied in my stay there.

Among those of us at the house, I noticed a wide age gap, with the youngest being twenty-one (me) and the oldest being in his seventies. I felt, though, that this wasn't just a normal gathering, but rather that these other people had come here because of a genuine interest in meeting Ali's newfound friend. As I usually found in situations like this, it didn't take long for the conversation to turn to more serious matters. There definitely wasn't much talk about the local sporting teams, the stupid thing someone's wife did the other week, or who was going to get eliminated from *Kitchen Nightmares* on TV next week. There were much bigger issues to talk about. Maybe it could have been because I wouldn't have had any relevance to the other types of conversation, but I felt pretty sure it was just the way things were around there. And rightly so. I wanted to learn and ask some questions that I had, but at the same time, I didn't want to take the chance of bringing the mood down on what seemed like such a lovely occasion.

So I proceeded to innocently to put forth a questions in a way that implied I was poking a little fun at the Israelis: "What do you think of the Israelis putting up so many walls? It's a bit extreme, isn't it?"

Ali immediately jumped in with his response, while everyone else turned their attention to him in a most serious way to hear his answer.

"No, not really," Ali said. "It is something I can actually understand from their point very well. This section of the wall was completed only a few months ago. Before this, for years, there have been between three to four suicide bombings per month on average, originating in this region of the West Bank, killing or injuring close to eighty Israelis every month. Now, since the completion of the wall, there have been none. This in turn does something very important for us. It stops retaliation. If the extremists in these parts cannot reach their target, then there is no retaliation from Israel and our innocents don't die.

"Although I say this, there is the other side, as there always has been the two sides in this conflict. There is so much disruption to our way of life, though, because where they build the wall, it interrupts our homes and businesses. Some are removed and the infrastructure is disturbed. And unfortunately, they cannot see that these sort of acts of destroying our infrastructure are ultimately going to come back on to them, because it will only breed more extremism and they cannot build walls high enough to stop a rocket."

*Wow,* I thought. *I'm not really going about this the right way. My first question, and I have already brought the conversation on to a level of death and destruction.* So I thought I would drop that touchy subject and try a different angle.

"So, Ali, I can't help but notice you are bit of a rock star around here. People seem to not only know who you are everywhere we go, but seem to admire and respect you. Why are you so popular? How do so many people know

198

you? And why do they seem to look up to you so much?"

And then it came back: that seriousness I had tried to tiptoe around. It came flooding right back into the room when Ali began to speak.

"Adam," he said. "I am an honest man, so I will tell you the truth. Twenty years ago, some other 'activists' and I planted a bomb that killed three Israeli soldiers. I was in jail for many years because of this. That is one reason why people know me and respect me around here."

*Uh-oh, what have I gotten myself into here?* I thought.

"But you have nothing to fear, my friend," Ali said, likely reading the concern on my face.

I don't know why, but although it came as a little bit of a shock to me, I didn't feel a sudden rush of fear. Ali is another example of what I have learned about similarities among people all over the world. Out of all of the people who do high-level criminal acts like this, 99 percent of them are just like you and me. You could be friends with them, have similar interests, and laugh together. But sometimes there is a slightly different belief (as there always is) that gets installed in their minds. When a slightly different belief turns into be an extremist belief, well, that is what separates us. Somehow, the animalistic, Neanderthal instinct of "Kill or be killed" gets triggered, and we live with an attitude of "an eye for an eye," and preservation for ourselves and our family. In my opinion, that is the only thing that makes us different in the radical sense. It's not the white knight versus black knight, evil versus good, clean-cut and physically fit hero versus the scraggy and long-haired ogre that we are brought up to believe, which society declares intentionally to dissociate us from each other in the humane sense. It isn't that clearly defined in life, though.

"Why did you do it?" I asked.

"At the time, I was very young, and I got caught up

199

in the struggle. I was doing my part, and I thought that it was the part I should be playing. Something swelled inside of me. It started with pride and then turned into courage, as I thought it would separate me from the others I thought didn't have the strength to do something like this. I wanted to send a message to the Israelis and they got it."

"Don't you regret having a hand in killing those people?"

"My friend," he replied. "Regret, no. But if I could take it back, I would. I am much older and wiser now. I realize that was not the answer and not the way to go about these things. But what's done is done. All that 'an eye for an eye' leads to is a vicious circle of vengeance, death, and loss. In no way have I lost passion or enthusiasm for my people's struggle, though. If anything, it has intensified because I know it is not so black and white anymore, as I somewhat believed it was back then. Today, I still fight for our struggle, but in a very different way. I do it through the right means. I meet people like you, and I know our story will be told and heard by more when you leave. I teach the young generations that the only way we can and should stop this cycle is to do it through peaceful means. We don't have resources to fight a war, nor will it do anything but breed more hatred. I try to help people not just in mind, but in body as well. For instance, I helped establish Ambulances for Human Rights, a project organized by both Palestinians and anti-Zionist Israelis [who are more in number than many may believe] to come to the defense of Palestinians under attack. We send mobile car units to go to the assistance of the Palestinians wounded by Israeli gunfire. This is still a small but significant effort. But it is a start."

"Ali is correct," another man said. "We look up to Ali not because of what he did or the way he did it, but because of the way he has been from one side of the river to the other, and then against the current he has once again

200

swum back. There are many who have taken up the extremist plight, as we call it, and many who have seen it from the non-extremist point of view followed by the extremist. But to swallow your pride and go back again afterward is something to be admired. And what we have seen and a lot of people realize in Palestine through their own struggles, is that we need to make the children see without having to go through the extremist points of view."

"Why do you think that is the case? The reason why so many are seemingly taken through the extremist point of view here?" I asked.

"Because children will be shaped by the environment they are raised in," the man said. "As an example, if the most precious thing in a child's life is taken away from them—their parents—why would they not be filled with hatred and want revenge? So the extremists teach the children that if they are a martyr, they will go to heaven and be with God. There, they will have everything they want, including their family, so why would they want to live in this shit?"

I nodded, then asked, "So how do you take the children out of this?"

"The only way is to teach them the virtues: patience, tolerance, understanding, and forgiveness. Extremism is a very hard thing to spread when people are not oppressed, but as soon as they are, it will spread like wildfire. And by teaching these things, you will take the oppression out of one's heart, which is the fundamental start."

"And how does it come to this?" I asked. "I mean, don't get me wrong, I know that the land that is now Israel came to be in this state fifty years ago when the British made it an independent country and gave it to the Israelis. But how has something like this in this day and age gone on for so long?"

Another man who had been listening now jumped

into the conversation: "Those who rule on both sides have their own agendas. And, unfortunately, although they may believe otherwise, it involves less than 10 percent of the population on their respective sides. They twist words and make the people believe in what they want because they think they know what is best for all. They think they can put everyone in one corner of the room and manipulate them into getting along and agreeing on everything. They think they live amongst us, but in truth, they rarely have the struggles that most of the population under their control endure. It is the same on the other end as well. For example, the 5 percent of people in Palestine that are misled and end up throwing 'stones,' to which the Israelis reply with great force, affects all of us as a whole. It makes the other 95 percent of us a target as well. So there you have it, the top minority and bottom minority of a population screwing everything up for the majority. It is wrong on both sides on so many different levels, but there is an easy solution. In my opinion, let the people from both sides and all echelons be neighbors, let the children play, let us integrate together, and let us be human."

I nodded again. "You are exactly right," I said. "I guess it is the same in a lot of places—well, everywhere really, in one form or another, because an economy is ruled by possession, whether it be money in capitalism or food within a tribe. More possession gives you a different life from the rest of the people. And that possession also gives you power. So you are the ruling elite who are out of touch with the rest of the population, so how are you supposed to make a hard decision on someone's behalf when you know nothing of the situation? And you are too easily corrupted because you are neither emotionally involved or have to feel a great extent of repercussions if the wrong choice is made?"

Everyone in our circle nodded in agreement to my comments—except one man. I had been keeping a keen eye on the circle throughout the conversation, and I had noticed the seemingly disagreeable look that this one man had on his face for most of the evening. His expression seemed one of open-mindedness, but I could just tell that he had been through some hard times and he seemed bitter—twisted and filled with deep-seated hatred.

I decided to see what he had to say. "And tell me, my friend," I said to the man, "what is your opinion on this matter? I am curious to know, as you don't look like you agree entirely."

"The Israelis are willing to pick up weapons and fight, but we have the advantage because we are willing to die. It always is the balance between the oppressors and oppressed. And like in conflicts all over the world, we will never know when we have been conquered, because these days, we all know that there is no quality of life ruled by oppression, and where are we to go if we can't live on our own land? No, we will fight, and we may die, but the dogs will never get the best of us because they will not stop until we are either no more or we are their slaves."

"Please forgive me, my friend, if I seem out of place, but may I say something?" I asked.

"Yes, of course, we are all friends here."

"What you speak of here sounds like pride. It is up to you to be the bigger person, to be the bigger man, and stop the hatred. Like Mandela, like Martin Luther King. Surely history has taught us that this is how great victories in battles like this are won—and in every circumstance, won with less violence because it appeals to the human nature of the oppressors unlike violence ever could."

"A leopard cannot change its spots," the man said. "I, for one, will not be frightened into submission."

"Well," I said, "if you yourself cannot forgive, surely you can love your children enough to teach them forgiveness. Therefore, the hatred will slowly die and revenge will not be sought on both sides, and the cycle will

203

end, eventually leading to peace for all—if it is indeed peace you want and not vengeance."

"These dogs will not stop until we are vanquished from our homes and lands," the man said.

"So tell me, where does the cycle end, then, because if they are winning the war, why would they change their tactics? A winning team will not change its course of action. It is up to the losing side to change something in the way the game is being played to turn it around. It's like Ali has taught me in my short time with him: it is up to you. How else do you stop the cycle? Someone shoots a rocket into Israel. They retaliate and destroy infrastructure, build walls, and innocent lives are lost. In itself, this is simple mathematics: you lose a hundred times more people than they do.

"People here lose their jobs because borders close and the economy goes down. People here get angry, which is born out of frustration, despair, poverty, and being destitute, because their family is starving. Mind-sets are changed from the one of innocence we all have as children, and people get desperate, so hope in extremism is found." I shrugged. "It's human nature. It's the same reason a man buys a lottery ticket in the West: hope, not realism. Then this false hope makes someone shoot a rocket into Israel."

Ali looked over at me and smiled. He had been sitting there observing me while listening to the debate I had been having with his friend. I had wondered why he had not stepped into the conversation before this, as half of everything I had been saying came from what he had shown and told me. Then it dawned on me. This was his point. He was silent because, in his mind, he had just educated another person who would pass the message on and keep the momentum of the plight of the Palestinian people going in a positive, yet passive way.

/////

The next morning, it was time to leave and go back to

Jerusalem, where I would be staying for one more night before heading to Haifa to stay with Sergei. At this point, I felt high on life and filled with hope because of the experiences I'd had over the past couple of days. But, unfortunately, as I was leaving, I had a very sobering experience that reminded me once again of where I was and the situation all around me.

One of the men from the house was going to Jerusalem that day, so he offered to give me a lift all the way to Jerusalem. Ali had decided to stay behind until the next day to take care of some things, as he put it. So we left Ramallah and headed back to the border post. Once in line, I noticed that two Israeli soldiers approached a car about three vehicles in front of us. The Israeli soldiers crept forward and had their machine guns held in front of them instead of slung on their backs. All of the sudden, the car took off and sped around the border post. The Israelis opened fire, and little bursts of glass shot out of car's back window as it was peppered with bullets. It didn't take long for the car to start losing momentum and then come to a halt. The car jerked to a stop in a little ditch on the side of the road. A young man jumped out of the passenger side and ran across the field. Three more shots rang out as I was watching from not more than forty meters away. I saw the young Palestinian go limp and his lifeless body flopped to the ground—no screaming, no movement. I could tell by the way he fell that his life force had completely gone from him. He was dead before he even hit the ground.

I feared the worst for the driver of the car, and I wanted to see if he was okay, but every bone in my body told me to stay in the car and not do anything. The rest of the line of cars was hurried through the border, It was then immediately closed and it was all over just like that.

*(NOTE: After I left Israel and returned to the UK, I did some research on the Internet for Ali Jiddah. Much has*

*been written about him, and he's also featured in several videos. If you'd like to know more about this fascinating man, I encourage you to go online and see for yourself.)*

# CHAPTER 19

# WONDERS OF THE MIDDLE EAST

I arrived in Haifa on the bus to find Sergei standing there waiting patiently for me. He was and imposing figure, standing about six-two, with a solid, square build and broad shoulders. He had a chiseled jaw that looked like it could take more than a few punches—and looked like it had at various stages during his life. He was Russian born and bred, as I mentioned before, and when he was twenty-two (almost the same age I was at the time), he'd moved to Israel to escape a life of little prospects and hope for a bright future, as well as having to deal with corruption on a regular basis. He'd decided to come to Israel because he knew that if he volunteered for military service there, he would be granted citizenship after five years. It was much easier than trying to immigrate to Europe or any other Western countries, being a Russian native. Sergei had learned some English in Russia from watching Western movies and listening to music in English (this is quite common in Russia and various other countries where the schools don't teach English). He studied Hebrew in Israel and became conversational in about six months. He also completed an engineering degree, and then during his time in the military, he completed his master's degree. He was now twenty-seven, out of the military and working at the Technion Israel Institute of Technology.

The Technion in Haifa is the oldest university in Israel, renowned throughout the world as an institute for engineering and the sciences. It has also had various Nobel prize laureates work there. So, needless to say, it is a prestigious place, and Sergei was a smart man indeed.

Sergei lived in a one-bedroom apartment in a fairly

nice area of Haifa. But, saying that, it seemed (from the areas I saw, at least) that there weren't too many run-down areas of the nation as a whole—apart from the "Palestinian territories," so to speak, which came across as run-down, dilapidated, and obviously severely underfunded.

Sergei's home was full of books, some in English, some in Hebrew, and some in Russian. He had hundreds of them, and they varied in topics: psychology, physics, biology, travel, literature, philosophy, physiology, sociology, and various books on economic systems such as socialism, Marxism, capitalism, etc.

Everything throughout his whole home, including the bookshelves, was neatly organized and categorized. Everything looked like it was where it should be. His clothes were pressed and neatly folded, his bed made and with the corners matching up to millimeter precision. Even his fridge, which although sparse with food, was neatly divided into dairy, vegetable, and meat sections. Sergei was an interesting person to meet. I was still trying to get my head around the fact that only a week or so ago he had met me as a complete stranger in Egypt, invited me to his home, had made sure I got there, picked me up, and even gave up his bed for me. He didn't have much room in his apartment, either, and he didn't have a spare mattress. So he got a bunch of sheets and towels from his linen cupboard and made himself a bed on the floor right next to his usual one. I tried to tell him that I would sleep on the floor, but he insisted to the absolute finite degree that he would be ashamed of himself if he invited someone into his home, then made them sleep on the floor. I truly felt sorry for him, because it really didn't look comfortable and his real bed was a 30cm-thick proper spring mattress—and he obviously knew how comfortable it was. The few days I was there, he went out of his way to make sure I had everything I needed. I even remember making a joke one time about how it had been the longest I had gone without having sex for years. To which, he immediately replied, "Although I do not use them myself, I could get you a prostitute."

"No no! I was joking! I have a girlfriend," I said.

Then, in the traditional Jewish manner, Sergei proceeded to explain: "Well, my friend, it is a very natural thing. Every male needs it, and if some men can't get it, there is absolutely nothing wrong with him paying for it. As far as the woman is happy to be receiving money for it, then there is nothing wrong with the act."

*Wow,* I thought. I had never heard it put so plainly before, and to be honest, the concept of it had never seemed so straightforward and acceptable to me before. However, it still wasn't something I wanted to participate in.

Although Haifa wasn't exactly a main tourist destination, Sergei took it upon himself to be my personal tour guide in addition to being my host. He took me to the Technion where he worked, and through him, I was able to access certain labs and meet some professors, which I wouldn't have otherwise been able to do.

We also went to the Sea of Galilee, where the famous story of Jesus feeding the five thousand with five loaves of bread and two fish was said to have taken place. It's also where he calmed a storm to save some fishermen's lives, and he also walked on the water there.

One of the most interesting experiences I had in Haifa was when we went to a few little cafes and bars that only a local would know about, and Sergei introduced me to some of his friends and colleagues. I distinctly remember a conversation that I had with one of his friends in one bar. It started off as your normal, formal " meet and greet" conversation: "Where are you from? What do you? etc." It didn't take long, though, for us both to become a little more comfortable and familiar with each other, and the conversation loosened up a little. When I was comfortable with our newfound level of conversation, I decided to ask

209

him his opinion about various heated subjects, which for some people in Israel and around the world were touchy subjects. I wasn't too sure how he would respond to such questions. But to my surprise, he was more than willing to discuss them in an open manner in that public place.

I asked him about military conscription, and his opinion was that he and most of the people he knew were against it. But at the same time, because of the politics of the Israeli government, the people are led to believe they are under constant threat, and most of the time actually are. So, without conscription, they would have no one to guard the borders and keep the mass population safe from: the consequences of their own government's military actions, and the genuine threat of extremist groups such as Hamas.

We also talked about the Palestinian people and the ongoing war. With this, he tiptoed around the subject a little before explaining to me that the war and hatred had been going on for so long that no one even remembered why they were fighting anymore. It was really a case of people trying to get revenge for their ancestors being wronged or a friend of a friend of a friend in the past, and it all just added up to a vicious cycle o f hatred and death.

He told me he personally had no specific hatred for any individual, but strongly disliked what the Palestinians stood for as a group. But, even saying that, he understood how they would fight back and rebel against what sometimes would come across as oppression by Israel. He also admitted he would do the same if he was in their shoes. From an Israeli point of view, he knew he had to stand there and sometimes shoot first to protect his country and family. At the same time, though he, was confident that, if left to their own devices, 90 percent of both the Israeli and Palestinian populations could get along just like any others. Then, with re-education of the first 90 percent, another 9 percent could be shown that there was no need for the hatred and violence. As for the remaining people,

210

though ... "Well, my friend, there will always be assholes everywhere," he said.

"Here," he went on, "let me tell you a story that my father told me a few years ago. It was a valuable lesson for me and thankfully one I learned without violence. Maybe one day, you can tell this story to others, and if it only makes one person stop and think, then it is enough, because it is another person that will share the story.

"I worked for about three years in a factory in Israel, just on the outskirts of the border to Gaza. Every day, workers from Gaza used to come over and work in the same factory. We would share jokes with each other, talk about our time off and what we did with our children. We would even complain about our wives to each other. And with those whom I became close friends with, we would even complain about and joke behind the back of the other workers, both Israeli and Palestinian, that we didn't get along with.

"We all had a common purpose in that place. We all had to work together as a team, and through that, we all got along to an acceptable degree. Everyone was an individual, and when you break people down to their individualism, they break out of the mold of all the stereotypical reasons that we are taught to hate each other about. They become human, they lose their race and religion, and you see just how similar we all are when you take away these stereotypes that society puts in place.

"But, unfortunately, not everyone could see things in this light. And a young man who had been taught hatred by someone who had learned it from someone else decided to seek glory in a cause that he didn't understand, but was told he didn't need to. He came to that factory, and he blew himself up, injuring many people. Although by the grace of God, no innocent people lost their lives, there were other repercussions. Palestinians were not allowed to come to work in the factory anymore, so we both lost friendships.

211

They lost their jobs, which affected their families. But most importantly, another way for all those people to gain tolerance and understanding toward each other was extinguished."

I listened as he went on to express his opinion about the leaders of the country and how he thought they had been caught up in an outdated idealism of how one group of people could be such an integral part of the world but at the same time separate themselves from other races, creeds, and religions to form a utopian society in the middle of an otherwise chaotic world. And how the politicians were so far removed from the reality of what the general masses of the population were about and what they wanted. It was "like an exclusive boys-only club where the opinion of things had always been the same and always will be, so even though our ways haven't worked, let's do things the way we always have," he said of the attitudes of these politicians. "We know what is best for the people; they are just too naïve to see otherwise."

He even told me a few stories about his time in the military, how he had lost a friend in a suicide bombing on the border, and how he had once shot at a man and saw him go down. I asked if he killed him.

"I don't know," he said. "It is possible, but you try not to think about these things so much. It is just a job at the end of the day, really, even though sometimes it seems like we have guns and they have stones, which a lot of the time this is true. We would have our machine guns and they would be throwing stones. It was a true interpretation of David and Goliath. We are told that, for the most part, it is a world there of kill-or-be-killed. Maybe not today, maybe not tomorrow, but without discipline, these people will grow into bombers and terrorists. This is how it is on the front line. These are the words that are repeatedly instilled in us, and if you tell someone something often enough, they will be forced to believe it. It is not until we return home that our minds can be cleared and we can see differently."

# CHAPTER 20

## UTOPIAN DREAMS

About a week into my stay with Sergei, Nadav came up with a suggestion that we all go to a party that his friend had invited us to. Never one to shy away from a party, I more than eagerly jumped at the chance to go to an Israeli house party, mingle with some more locals, and have more than my share of beers.

The next day, we left early in the evening and arrived at the party about seven o'clock. I wasn't sure at first, because the drive there didn't really seem like we would be going to a place that would have a house, let alone a house party. We drove through the city and then out into the countryside, past what seemed to be farming area and then into a forested area. We took a turn off the main road, down a long dirt driveway. I definitely would have been a bit nervous if I hadn't gotten so comfortable around and trusting of Sergei over the past couple of weeks. When we arrived at the end of the road, it opened up into what could be described as a normal suburb on the outskirts of any city, although it wasn't near a city.

"This is a strange setup," I said. "All this out in the middle of nowhere."

It didn't even dawn on me where we were until Nadav said, "So you have never been to a kibbutz before? This will be a different experience for you, then."

I had always heard about kibbutzim, but didn't really have a complete understanding of what they were, so I was about to find out for myself firsthand.

We drove through the "suburb" and arrived at a massive shed on the edge of some farmland. At least a hundred people were socializing and enjoying themselves there. We got out of the car and joined in the festivities. Nadav introduced me to the friends of his that he knew.

"Shalom," they said to me, which is the typical Hebrew greeting for both "Hello" and "Good-bye."

I replied with the same.

"Where are you from, friend?" one of them asked.

"Australia," I replied.

"You are very welcome here. I am surprised and must know how you managed to come here all the way from Australia. You have to tell me the story."

At this stage, a couple more of his friends had come over and joined to settle their curiosity me as a stranger and what I was doing there. So I proceeded to tell the story of how I had come on holiday from the UK, and had met Sergei and Nadav in Egypt and they had invited me to stay with them.

"Well, that is fantastic," the man said. "And there is only one thing I should do really, and that is extend the hospitality even further and invite you to stay here for a couple of days. What do you say? You can stay in my house and live on a kibbutz for a little while. I know that if you don't know what one really is, it will be an interesting experience for you, I think."

"Yes, please," someone else said. "It would be great."

And feeling so welcomed, it wasn't long into the night after a few drinks that I finally accepted the offer.

So Sergei and Nadav left later that evening and planned to come back to pick me up whenever I was ready to leave.

I spent the next while living the life of someone whom spends all of their time in a kibbutz. It was quite literally a self-contained community. These days, kibbutzim are based around all sorts of industry, from basic factory work to even high-tech and military industries. This one, though, was based around a more traditional form:

215

agriculture.

People would get up in the morning and seemingly at first live their lives the same ways as we did in the West. So I got up bright and early with my host Oren, and although I wasn't expected to, I helped out doing various odd jobs. I helped repair someone's front steps, I played with some kids for a while, I helped carry some building materials, and I spent part of my day hand-digging some irrigation ditches. The greatest thing about spending my time helping out like this was that it gave me an opportunity to talk to the people in the community and to learn more of what they and this style of living were all about.

I found it quite fascinating to learn about the inner workings of a kibbutz. I was told that they originally started at the turn of the twentieth century, the purpose being to form a utopian community by way of a combination of socialism (based on the idea of communal ownership) and Zionism. Zionism is an extremely pro-Jewish-cultured society, even to the extent that assimilation by other peoples into society is frowned upon and migration of Jews into other countries is strongly discouraged. Even whole families are encouraged to return and live in Israel. This to a great extent is still encouraged today. For example, there is something known as the Jewish birthright, which means basically wherever you are in the world, if you were born to at least one Jewish parent (along with a few other minor criteria), you get a free trip to Israel, all expenses paid to visit the homeland. At the time I was there, they told me that these Jewish visitors would be bombarded with religion and persuaded to stay, even to the extreme of encouraging alcohol and sex to try to "increase" the Jewish community. The more I thought and heard about Zionism, the more it dawned on me that the hostel I'd stayed at in Jerusalem was one of these places.

I was amazed at how enforced and highly regarded

the principal of equality was in the community as well. I was told that up until recently, people in the community did not individually own tools, or even clothing. Gifts and income received from outside were turned over to the common treasury. If someone received a gift in services, it was frowned upon and thought to be morally wrong to accept it. Everyone up until recently (due to the size of the community) even ate meals together in a massive dining hall.

The only reason that women were thought to be different from men was the fact that they gave birth to the children. Besides that, they were not in any way tied or obligated to be a part of the domestication of the household or the raising of the children. In fact, the upbringing of the children was completely different. The children would spend most of their time learning, playing, and sleeping in a communal children's house. Parents spent three to four hours a day in the afternoon with their children after work and before dinner. That was it, but when you think about it, that's a lot more quality time that they get to spend together than in most societies.

Because of this separation between parents and children, I learned that children did not view their parents as strict authority figures, and it was more of a general "Adults are older and wiser, so should be listened to" instead of that strict "Mum and Dad's word is law" feeling to it. Also, it meant that the children didn't have to rely on the parents economically, socially, or for any other means. As for the parents, this way of interaction apparently eliminated the tendency to look at their children as possessions and to possibly restrict them from growing into their own persons.

There are also few instances of crime on a kibbutz. Since everyone has their basic needs taken care of and everything is communally shared, there is really no reason for theft.

Over those few days, I became convinced that this was a perfect way to live, that it was indeed the utopian society that it had claimed to be. But, not wanting to be naïve, I always kept an ear and mind open to the occasional story that would swing the other way. I woke up a little and slowly came to realize a few things, and this new line of thought came about because of something one of the elderly men said to me. He had been living on the kibbutz for forty years.

"It is not for everybody," he said. "To many, people don't want to make the sacrifices they need to make to live this life in a utopian society. Most people who know different will eventually succumb to the basic human instinct and urge to accumulate the three P's: power, privilege, and prestige. And with that, it always seems to gravitate more toward a Western society every time.

"For instance, thirty years ago, both men and women were equally rotated into different jobs. One week, a person might work in planting, the next with livestock, the week after in the laundry. Even managers would have to work in menial jobs. Through rotation, people took part in every kind of work, but it interfered with any process of specialization, which ultimately made the society suffer. For example, it takes years to learn to be a good carpenter, doctor, or cheese-maker. Individuals need to invest time in one thing to become a master at it. You have two choices. You either let this happen, or you live with cheese that doesn't taste as good, steps that you might trip upon, and a doctor that might misdiagnose your child's illness. And no community wants their children to suffer.

"There are more complex problems like this that arise through everyone trying to be equal. For a first example, it is impossible for us to make everything we need. There aren't the resources. So we need to make more of our product to sell so we can have money to buy the other things we need. For example, in agriculture, you need more people at harvest time than are available in the community. You need seasonal workers to fill these positions so the rest of the labor force in the community isn't stretched to breaking point. So you look elsewhere. You bring foreigners in for the season, and they have their influences and don't necessarily want to lead the communal life, which causes drama and segregation. Then the young want to leave because the grass is always greener on the other side.

"Then, for a second example, you get some children who grow up to be extra special, and to help them flourish, they need to go to a college to train their mind. So they in turn are in the outside world and gather influences from that. And when they have their degree in engineering or whatever it is, there just aren't those jobs available here, so they end up working in the cities. Yes, their money comes back to the community, but that person needs more than the rest of the people in the community: money for gas and a car to drive to work, a suit, etc. Which brings inequality back into the society and undermines the whole foundation of what we have built this upon. It is great, but once again, like all society structures, it is flawed and there are always inequalities produced because of our human nature."

As I thought about this, I couldn't help but ask a question that had been burning a hole in the back of my mind for a while, but I hadn't asked because I thought it might come across as a little rude.

"I'm not sure," I said, "it might just be me, but correct me if I'm wrong. Everyone seems a little bit flat here. There almost seems to be a little something missing. I noticed that I haven't heard anyone overjoyed or at all emotionally ecstatic about anything while I have been here."

He nodded. "Yes, I know what you mean. There have been studies done on this very thing you ask. There is a wide belief that, in childhood, having possessions helps us grow our emotions, jealousy, envy, love, hope, all of them. And without the presence of possessions, the development of these emotions is marred, which changes the whole outlook of things on other aspects of life."

I knew that my belief of the kibbutz being a perfect society might have been crashing down at that moment.

"Wow," I said. "It seems like there are just as many bad points as good points to this way of living. Why do you stay?"

"Well, I have been here for a long time. I moved here when I was maybe twenty, and compared to what I moved away from, this was indeed a utopian existence. But, over time, I came to realize these things, among others that I just explained to you, were major problems with this way of existence. I have been here too long to learn any different. This is the way I know and accept now. But also, really, at the end of the day, what society is perfect? Even your capitalism is far, far from perfect. Yes, you have more freedoms than any other social structure, but the divides it creates are astronomical. The massive gaps between rich and poor. The loss of the meaning of community. Drug problems, corruption problems, the list goes on, really.

"No, that is not a place for me. Since I know this so well, the best thing for me is to do what all whom are given the freedom to do so should try to do: slowly and carefully change the society they live in so it may be better for the next generations. Society structures are things that need to be constantly worked on, tweaked, and changed, because the changing of the social norms and rules in society should change people for the better. And when people change for the better, the rules need to change to accommodate new problems that may arise because of it."

With a head full of new thoughts on life, I went on with kibbutz life until Sergei came to pick me up in the evening later on that week. We ended up staying for a bit while I told Sergei about the events of the past days and while he socialized with his newfound friends of a couple of days ago. In fact, time ended up getting away from us, and we didn't end up leaving until about four o'clock in the morning. As we were driving back to his house, we saw a couple of young girls hitchhiking on the side of the road. Because they were walking alone in the somewhat middle of nowhere, Sergei proceeded to pull over. The two couldn't have been older than sixteen.

Apparently, I was the only one who thought this a little strange: two men in their twenties pulling over early in the morning to give a lift to a couple of underage girls.

"A lot of people do it here," Sergei told me when he noticed my curiosity.

Apparently from growing up in Russia, he also knew that this wasn't a practiced thing all over the world.

"From ten-year-olds to eighty-year-olds, it doesn't matter who needs a lift. It is about helping people out."

And then I realized it was Western society that had given it such a big stigmata. Our society in a way had lost a sense of community and helping each other out. Somehow it had managed to breed a culture of fear into us about doing something so simple like this. But, granted, it was because that Western society of ours had once again managed to breed a few people who took advantage of situations like this and had preyed on the innocence of others, which concluded in horrendous outcomes. It was a shame that the west had to be like this, but to sort out a problem like that, you would have to delve even deeper and get to the root of the problem: Western society itself.

Two days later, it was unfortunately time to finally leave Israel and head to Jordan. It had been a mind-opening experience, and I felt that so much had happened in such a relatively short amount of time. I left with a sense of bewilderment, but mostly in a positive way. It seemed like they had everything the same as the West, but to more extremes. The dangers were more dangerous, ever present, and far more extreme. But on the other end of the scale, maybe somewhat due to these things, there was a greater sense of safety in a lot of aspects, and more trust could be placed in each other and situations. It kind of felt like if you were to take your car to a mechanic in Israel, it wouldn't come back with more problems than you took it there with.

Even as I left Israel, though, my thoughts of the dangers there would quickly come back to the forefront of my mind.

A suicide bombing occurred on October 4, 2003, in the beachfront Maxim restaurant in Haifa. Twenty-one people were killed in the attack and fifty-one were injured. Among the victims were two families and four children, including a two-month-old baby. The attack took place just days after I left the city.

Although the interior of the restaurant was completely destroyed in the attack, it was quickly rebuilt and reopened within several months. A monument was erected near the restaurant in memory of the victims killed in the attack, and my thoughts still often go back to the reality of the dangers of where I had been in Israel and Palestine.

# CHAPTER 21

## OPENING OF THE EYES

I had once again moved on and knew no one in Jordan. The solitude of traveling can sometimes be the hardest thing to deal with. But that solitude also gives you the freedom to basically do whatever you want whenever you want. You can wake up in the morning and choose whatever direction you desire, or you can sleep in that morning. It's up to you.

Arriving at the bus depot in Amman, I once again found myself in that awkward position of not knowing but needing—as in not knowing anyone there, not knowing where I was going, and not knowing what I was to do, but at the same time, needing a place to stay, needing to communicate in a foreign language, and needing to have my wits about me. I was also only 300km from the Iraqi border, 150km from the Saudi border, and, well, generally in a region of the world that seemed from the outside to not be so hospitable given the current climate. But, contrary to what most people would probably think, the locals were open and friendly. Probably even more surprising was the fact that the most friendly people I met were the Iraqis. And there were hundreds of them, all fleeing west from the turmoil happening back home. They were coming to Jordan to start a new life.

Over the couple of days I explored Amman, I would say probably ten people came up to me, just wanting to shake my hand, ask me where I was from, and say thank you for what my country was participating in, as the US-Allied invasion of Iraq had happened only five months ago. Tourism was a little bit down, I guess you could say, being so close to Iraq and all.

These people were in stark contrast to a lot of

stories that you would hear and assume in the West—stories that you hear of people who think that the invasion was just a ploy by the West to come and rape Iraq for its natural resource wealth ... something that is more than overfed in popular social media these days. The reality was clearly shown to me by all the handshakes and stories I heard about how people had suffered under the genocidal regime of Saddam Hussein.

That's a strange thing that I have found about Westerners who hate their governments and the societies they live in: the ones who slag them off, accuse them of looking after no one's interest but the elites, the so-called anarchists who blame the government institution rather than what actually is a few people who make corrupt decisions.

A small part of the time, these people can be like little children and get carried away without stopping and thinking. They turn into propagandists and spread hatred toward the very institution that is giving them the freedom to do so. Don't get me wrong: I think it is great when people stand up for something they believe in, and give their thoughts and opinions. But it's a problem when they force it upon others because they think they are some high and mighty enlightened one, rather than someone simply informing people and letting them make their own decision.

Like when you disagree with your parents when you're growing up. You have a disagreement and you hate them. They don't know any better, you think. They're just old and out of date. You yell at them, scream at them, maybe run away or throw something at them, and they punish you if you take it too far, to make you see that it's for your own good. It's not until you get older that you realize that their opinion is shaped through years of experience, like a government's collective experience, and you realize that although they are not perfect by any means, to a certain degree they are protecting us from ourselves

224

and real-world threats. Socialism/capitalism is the best form of government infrastructure in the world in my opinion, and the best there has been to date. If people took the time to stop and actually compare its track record to any other—Imperialism, Communism, Marxism, etc.—I think they would agree. Others work well in theory, like Communism, but social-capitalism is the best put into practice. It is far, far from perfect, but it is something that should not be overturned and thrown away. It should be worked on and developed.

In socialism/capitalism, you realize that you have the right to take a stand against them, protest against them, have your say, and even slander them without any repercussions for the most part. It is your right in this society that you hate so much to be able to do those very things. I know plenty of places where they would just cut off your head and be done with it, like Iraq.

So is it such a bad thing when a coalition force enters another country to free those people from this type of oppression?

Yes, a war has to be paid for, and it is in turn repaid by a country's resources. Yes, the loss of life can be a high toll on both sides. But just maybe it is all worth it in the long run, so their children's children don't have to live in fear, oppression, poverty, and with no hope for a bright future.

# CHAPTER 22

## ANOTHER ONE OFF THE BUCKET LIST

It wasn't too hard to find someone in Jordan that would drive me to all of the places that I wanted to go but were too far by foot. In fact, when checking into my hotel, the first thing the man at the counter said was, "Hello, my friend, do you need a driver as well for your stay?"

I was the only tourist I had seen so far and was sure he was trying to drum up some business for one of his family members. Still, I was more than happy to take up the offer after some not so aggressive negotiations on the price, knowing how they must have been struggling a little. The city wasn't too bad to get around, so I decided to explore on foot firstly and then in a couple of days have this guy drive me to the place I had mainly gone there for: the Dead Sea.

Amman itself has a unique layout, as I would discover by exploring it all on foot. Walking is the best way to get around a city in my opinion, because you can pause for the attention to detail. It seemed to me like Amman had been built on three hills and in the U-shaped valley that lay between them. The hills were dotted with old, sandy-white red buildings that looked like they'd been built from clay the same way they had been for thousands of years. Even the few modern buildings that I saw looked like they were made of the same materials. All the buildings had character and didn't appear to be built to the highest standards.

One of the highlights was the Roman amphitheatre. Standing there, it blew my mind that that the Romans had managed to stretch their influence that far two thousand years ago, knowing the technology of that day and age.

When I went to the Dead Sea, I don't know why,

but it wasn't like anything I had expected. It definitely wasn't a picturesque place. First off, it definitely looked more like a lake than a sea. It was surrounded by gray, metallic-looking mud, the hills were barren and dull, and it felt like you were in the middle of a desert. But it was the place of legend, and a location that many people had come to experience over thousands of years—to swim in the Dead Sea and rub some of that metallic mud on their bodies, which beauty shops around the world sold for hundreds of dollars for a little jar's worth.

When it came to the actual swim itself, I was warned by my driver that not everyone who went there found it a pleasant experience.

"Make sure it's not in your eyes," he said to me in his broken English.

"Okay, thank you, I will," I said.

With that, I gave him my camera and trusted him with the rest of my belongings (except for my bank cards and passport, which I had left hidden in the car. The car was a fair distance away, and I was confident I could run him down if he tried to abandon me and steal my things. Although, I felt in these parts that theft wasn't really a major issue f you were introduced to someone, especially when associated with a hotel.

I took off my shirt and started to wade in. It was a pretty decent temperature and wasn't anything out of the usual in the beginning. Then I felt a slight stinging sensation on my foot, then on my arm, then on my back. And it wasn't long before I realized that the reason why you float in the sea is because of the high iodine/salt content, and that stinging sensation was the literal salt being rubbed into my wounds. The little scratches I had on my body (from over-scratching mosquito bites) started to sting all at once. It was uncomfortable to say the least, but I blocked it out the best I could. I soon got used to the stinging and the discomfort slipped from my mind as I got to about chest height in the water. I proceeded to sit down like I was reclining backward into a recliner chair and was soon floating in the Dead Sea. The buoyancy was amazing. I had my knees, head, arms, and half of my chest out of the water all at once. The closest thing I could compare it to was lying on a waterbed.

And with that, I waved at the driver for him to take a photo as I sat there, floating and reading my book, which I had specifically taken with me to get that iconic cliché photo of being in a relaxed, reclined position, pretending nothing is out of the ordinary. He snapped the picture, and another item was crossed off the bucket list.

After that, the driver took me to a city called Al-Hasa, where I planned to spend a day or two as I thought about what to do next. The driver somehow knew the owner of one hotel, or so he told me. I presume it was more of him approaching the hotel, telling them he had brought my business there, and then taking a cut, which didn't bother me too much.

I went to my room and lay down. It was getting late and I was tired. As I was lying there, I started thinking of all the amazing things I had seen and done over the past few weeks, but felt like there was something missing more and more as the days went on. I started realizing I was sick of being alone, with people coming and going. I had a great time but wanted to again share my time with someone I cared for. I wanted to be with Louise.

So the very next day, I left. Over the next fifty hours, I caught a bus to Aqaba, followed by the ferry to Taba in Egypt, and then another bus all the way back to Cairo. There, I hopped on a plane and was on my way to Bath.

# CHAPTER 23

## LIFE-ALTERING DECISIONS

One of the main reasons we ended up moving down to Bath was because Louise's cousin Roy lived there. Although she would rarely admit it, I think she had a real longing to be around her family once again. Roy was a straight-down-the-line kind of man, a typical no-messing-around kind of guy. He was smart and knowledgeable, with a knack for being able to fix anything that was fixable. He had become the local handyman in the small village of Upper Wraxall in Chippenham, which is about thirty minutes from Bath.

The town was a beautifully quaint little place, with cobblestone walls running around the outside of houses built from stone. Roy's backyard was not only perfect for a fire and a BBQ with beers in the summer, but also went on to a couple of acres of open land where you could roam as you please. It was old and rustic with a real sense of history and hominess. His house had a cozy little fireplace in the sitting room, from which you could watch the winter weather pass you by out the front window. It all seems so perfect looking back on it now, as a lot of memories do in life, I guess, in hindsight.

After staying at Roy and his girlfriend Julie's house for about a week, Louise and I met a couple of neighbors who lived down the road from them. They had a converted loft in a detached building on their property and offered to rent it out to us. It was more like an old converted barn, actually. There wasn't anything downstairs, but you entered straight up a staircase to the top level, where it would open out into one large room; I would estimate about five by fifteen meters. It had a small little kitchen with a microwave, portable hob for cooking, and a fridge, all taking up a quarter of the space; a couch with a TV occupying another quarter; and the remaining half was taken up by a large double bed and a little open area. It also had a separate room at the back with a toilet and bath/shower. It was really good living there in the beginning. It was the first time in forever, really, that it felt like I had my own place, with my own space, separated from the rest of the world, like an apartment, like most people in life have as their normality.

With the village being so small, it wasn't long before everybody knew about our arrival, and with a bit of luck, there was some work going around. Louise got a job in a pub again, about a ten-minute drive away (and we had loan of one of Roy's cars since he and Julie had two but barely even used one). It was something Louise was good at and really enjoyed doing, and as a bonus, she would have off Sunday and Mondays, and during the week, her shifts would normally finish about 7:00 p.m. because she was on the morning/afternoon shift all of the time. This in turn gave us time together at home, since my boss was also accommodating. I would be given off Sundays and Mondays as well.

And as for my line of work, I was offered something on a different path and decided to take it. I now like to sarcastically call my job title there a "pallet technician." Basically, I worked in the shed of some guy's house. This Chris had made a small fortune in selling secondhand shipping pallets—the wooden platforms used for shipping just about everything from one place to another since the start of the Industrial Revolution. Chris would buy these pallets from truck drivers, farmers, and anyone that would bring them by. Depending on quality (wear and tear) and grade (max weight capacity), he would buy them for between £1-£4 each. Then he would repair them and sell them back to shipping businesses for around £8-£10 a pop. This may sound expensive for a wooden pallet but it was still only 70 percent of what they would cost new. Business was good, and one main reason was because companies realized it was too expensive to have drivers wait around for their pallets to be unpacked and then brought all the way back to them, so they would factor in the price of them to the cost of the goods shipped. To them, they were of one-off use, and to the companies that received the goods, they were of little to no use, but to Chris, it was easy money, especially considering all that went into the repair costs was a couple of feet of wood, maybe a wooden block or two, and the labor. And labor really didn't turn out to be much, given that I was getting paid around £50 a day and would repair maybe a hundred pallets a day, leaving Chris a tidy profit of about £400 a day for doing almost nothing.

It was definitely not a job for a rocket scientist: picking out a pallet from the broken pile; putting it on a bench; ripping off any broken slats with a crowbar; smashing out split blocks with a mallet, sledgehammer, reciprocating saw, or whatever means it took; putting a new one into place, then whacking a few nails in with the nail gun; and the only thing left to do after that was place it on the fixed pile. It did pay the bills, though, and it held my interest for a while, being something completely different from what I had been doing. It felt good to be doing physical labor and not having to deal with customers for a change.

I would rarely see Chris because of his various liver problems, and I believe I met him only twice in the couple of months I worked there. Still, I wasn't alone at that job for maybe half of the time. I also worked alongside Martin, who took care of the business for Chris, and he was also the one who got me the job, being Roy and Julie's immediate neighbor.

Martin and his wife Sherry were a very lovely couple. He was a tall, broad man, about six-four, and he had the kind of figure you could mistake for a bouncer's. So it seemed fitting that he had such a physical job for a living, but this wasn't actually his original chosen profession, as evidenced by where he and Sherry lived. Their lovely house had a swimming pool and atrium, a couple of guest rooms, and all the mod cons in a spacious surrounding. He actually used to be a corporate insurance investment guy, one of the big wigs who earned $300k-plus a year, but he gave it all up because of the moral dilemmas that his job would make him face, having to lie to people, doing anything to get them to invest for his bosses. He just wasn't cut out for it and decided to take the moral high ground and leave it for a more honest life. I considered this a very honorable trait that I didn't find much in people in the West because of the way people are too easily consumed by greed. Martin, though, was a kind man with a genuine heart; he was always full of energy, always had a smile upon his face, and always was thinking one step ahead to lay his quick wit down in front of you and crack a joke. You could just genuinely tell that he had an interest in people and their well-being. Martin and Sherry also had a young child whom Louise would babysit for a night or two here and there.

As for Louise and me, this was the first time we had somewhat of a "normal" setup that we could call home. We did have the house while working at the Three Pigs, but we still had to share the place. Here, we had our own space and own place. If we didn't want to do the dishes for a couple of days, we didn't have to, and no one would complain about it. We didn't live with the people we worked with, and we didn't work with each other. It was good for the first time to be able to have separate friends from one another—just people you could say certain things to and not have it come back to you, or even just to get an opinion in an unbiased way due to that friend not knowing the other person.

For the first time ever, we also had the freedom that a car brought. We could drive down to the shops if we wanted, or go visit Bath to other touristy places on our days off. Life seemed to be going well, and we fell into a nice little routine there for a while. We were tucked away in a small little village in the English countryside. We had good neighbors that we could call friends, and they were so closely knit that we found employment and a place to stay because of them. We would also be invited around to dinner and social occasions throughout the neighborhood (although 90 percent of the time, it was at Roy and Julie's anyway due to the fact that they loved to entertain in their backyard with bonfires, BBQs, and beer). We were part of all the little things that make a community special and that add a bit of interest and meaning to life—things you wouldn't normally notice until you are away from them for so long.

I remember the joy I felt more than a few times when I would come home after a hard day's work, the old "9:00 to 5:00," so to speak—or in this case, actually 8:00 to 4:00. I would normally be home about three hours before Louise, so I'd grab a beer, sit on the couch, and relax in front of the TV. I had never really had that kind of an opportunity before.

It was great while it lasted, but as they say, nothing lasts forever, and an event was about to happen that would change the both Louise and me personally, and our relationship forever.

We were lying in bed one Sunday morning, and I don't exactly recall what we were talking about, but I do remember Louise being a little bit off in the way she was acting—as she quite often did when she had something big and pressing weighing on her shoulders and she wanted to talk about it but didn't know how to bring it up. Usually, we would talk and she would answer my questions tentatively and shyly. She wouldn't make eye contact and would do little things like ignore me to frustrate and provoke me into raising my voice at her so she would in turn get angry at me, then be able to blurt what was on her mind. This time was different, though.

"I'm late," she finally snarled at me. She whipped her head around to look at me and gauge my first reaction. I don't know why, but I instantly knew what she was referring to.

"What do you mean?" I asked, for no other reason but to have another couple of seconds to think.

"I think I might be pregnant."

"Oh, really? What makes you think that?" I stupidly asked so as to try to stall a little longer.

"I told you, I'm late. I am three weeks overdue on my period."

"Well … don't worry about it for now. You've been late before, right, by a week or so?"

"Yes, but never this long. This is like twice as long."

I tried to brush it off the best I could because I didn't want to waver and show any sense of panic. I suggested she get a test from the shops and not to worry about it until we saw what the results were.

She rolled her eyes at me, as if to say, "I knew that's exactly what you would say. Why do I even bother sometimes? You're an ass."

A few days later, she got a test and it turned out positive. I still tried to do what I thought at the time was coming across as strong and reassuring, but in hindsight probably came across as unemotional and a little cold.

"Those things aren't always right, right?" I asked.

"No, but they're pretty spot on."

"We'll make an appointment at the doctor, then. They will be able to give us a definite answer, no?"

"Yeah, yeah."

A few days later, I came home to Louise sitting on

one corner of the bed. her feet flat on the floor, legs together, her posture as straight as it could be. Her hands were sitting in her lap, each of them gripping one side of a scrunched-up tissue. She turned and look at me.

"It's twins," she said. "What are we going to do?"

My heart sank a little as the reality of the situation kicked in, and I realized that a lot of people in the world would have loved to be in this situation. But we were just two kids on the other side of the world trying to play grown-up, so there was no way of denying the gravity of the situation now.

"I don't know," was my first response. "What do you think?"

My question fell on deaf ears as she squirmed a little where she was sitting.

I walked over and sat down beside her, but she just moved farther away.

"Hey, come on," I said as I moved closer and tried to put my arm around her.

She stood up and walked away.

I didn't get it. She was closing me out, twisting at my heart. I could feel the resentment toward me for some unknown reason.

"Why won't you talk to me?" I asked.

"Leave me alone, and don't you tell anyone about this. I don't want anyone to know."

I got up and walked out the door in utter confusion. I couldn't explain it. What had I done wrong—and what were we going to do? I started to walk down the only road in the village, thoughts racing through my mind. It didn't take me very long to get to the end of the road, and I paused, looked back, then I kept walking. I walked through a field and into a forest and wondered amongst the trees, all the time thinking of the situation.

I tried to block out the emotional part of the situation from my mind. I tried to think logically and rationally. I tried not to let my emotions get involved as I thought it through.

What would it be like to bring not one but two children into the world? There was no way I could financially support two children and a wife. *What kind of life could I give them?* But it kept creeping into my head that these are two beings who will grow into life. *These will be your children to show the world to, to protect and be a role model to.*

I tried to block it out as a stinging sensation crept through me.

We would have to go back to Australia and start everything from square one. We didn't even have a vehicle to get around, let alone a place to live or jobs to earn money. And there would be no time for education to be able to earn a better living in time. The work would be for minimum wage.

*It doesn't matter so much about money. Just as long as you have love, everything will be okay.*

I wanted to believe this, but the realist point of view I had been raised with crushed the emotions that I was feeling. Thoughts of anger raged through me as I screamed inside my head trying to battle a demon within. *People who say that shit have no idea! They don't live in the real world. It is a cruel world, not one full of happy endings and cotton candy, for God's sake.*

If only my realist point of view had been on the optimistic side and not that of a pessimist, things might have turned out differently.

I really didn't know what to do. I thought maybe it would help to speak to someone. I thought of talking to Roy, but I felt I couldn't as he was Louise's cousin and she didn't want anyone to know, so to speak to him about it would be the ultimate betrayal of trust, as he was family. I didn't really know anyone else that well … anywhere.

I thought of talking to Martin, but I felt I didn't

know him that well—and again the thought rang in my head: "Don't tell anyone."

Next I thought of talking to my father back home. He was straight, level headed, and a realist. If I told him anything, I knew he would never speak a word to any soul, including my mother if I asked him not to. He was the most trustworthy person anyone could ever meet in life if they wanted him to be. As I once again thought of Louise insisting "no one," I knew automatically what my father's response would be, at least I presumed I did: "Neither of you are ready in any sense of the word, to bring a child let alone two into the world. Not financially, not emotionally, not in any way."

I got home a few hours later to Louise lying in bed. She was pretending to be asleep, but I knew she was awake. I had come to the conclusion in my mind that through the way she had acted toward me and the vibe I had been getting from her over the past few weeks that deep down she thought the same way I did: pessimistically realistic, even though she couldn't bring herself to speak the words. I felt that it was up to me to say it because she didn't have the strength to.

"Maybe we should have an abortion," I said.

She rolled over and said nothing. It was a sleepless night.

Neither of us had to go to work the next day, but when I awoke, Louise was already gone. I didn't think much of it at first, but then the hours started to pass. I tried calling, but there was no answer. I tried texting, but there was no reply. Lunchtime came and went. Dinner came and went.

My mind was racing. I knew the car was still out there, as I had checked first thing, so there was only one place I knew she could be—and that was at Roy and Julie's. I wanted to go over there, but I knew she was there for a reason and I knew she wouldn't want me to be there, otherwise she would have said something.

Why was she locking me out so much? It felt like torture. Did she not think that this would have an effect on me too? Why couldn't she see I was going through this as well? Maybe I hid my emotions from her a little too well. But she knew that's the way I was; she knew that's how I dealt with things. And she knew that I wasn't a heartless bastard. I couldn't understand why she didn't seem to care.

I eventually got a text at about 8:00 p.m. that evening. It read: *"I'm at Roy's, staying here tonight."* And that was it. I texted back, telling her that I felt she was shutting me out and I couldn't stop thinking about it, and it had been on my mind ever since she told me she might be pregnant. But she didn't reply.

There wasn't much contact between us over the next couple of days. She stayed at Roy's for two nights and after that wouldn't come back until she knew I would be in bed.

Later in the week, I came home and Louise was finally there.

"My appointment is tomorrow," she said.

"So you've decided that's what we should do?"

"It was your idea!" she snapped.

My heart felt whiplashed by her words, all to the back of my rib cage in my chest.

"Okay, okay," I said. "Do you think this is the right thing to do?"

She didn't answer me, but I knew what she was thinking: this was what she wanted, and this was why she was taking it out on me so badly, because she wanted to be able to take any blame that she would have off of herself.

*My shoulders are broad. I can take it,* I thought. *I love her, and if that's what she needs to do to deal with it, then so be it.*

"Julie is going to take me tomorrow," she said.

I immediately thought of how she wanted "no one"

238

to know and how I had to squirm in silence for the past few weeks, but I said nothing so as to not start an argument.

"Soooo you don't want me to come with you?" I said.

"No, I don't" were the words she used to pierce my heart this time.

"Why not? Don't fucking shut me out!"

"Fine, whatever! Come, then," she said.

I felt like she was doing whatever she could to antagonize me and get back at me like this was all my fault.

It was silent in the car the next day. None of the three of us said anything—except for one comment Julie made: "If you need to talk about anything, Adam, just let me know," she said.

"Thanks," I replied.

I felt stunned, really. It was the first time that someone actually cared about me in this situation. But I knew I couldn't talk to her about it. She was lovely but she just wouldn't be the right person to do it with.

We arrived at the clinic and I went to hop out of the car.

"Wait here," Louise said. "I don't want you there." Her tone had all the authority that a prison guard would have over a prisoner, which is exactly what I felt like.

The guilt really weighed me down. I felt guilty that I couldn't be there for her, that she didn't want me there. I started to doubt myself as a person. *Maybe I'm looking at myself in the wrong light. If the person I love doesn't want me to be there in a time like this, if she doesn't want to talk to me about it, then what kind of man am I?*

So as Julie and Louise went in, I was left to my own devices in the car. I could see the look of pity that Julie had for me, but pity was the last thing that I wanted. I paced around outside of the car, smoking cigarette after cigarette trying to calm my nerves as the seconds seemed to pass like minutes and the minutes in turn seemed like hours.

239

*Is this the right thing?* I thought.

I texted Louise and told her that we didn't have to do this, and maybe we should take more time to think about it. I received no answer.

A war started inside of my head between the optimist and the pessimist, the pragmatist versus the idealist, the devil on one shoulder and the angel on the other.

*Why do I feel like so much of this was my decision? Why was so much weight put on my shoulders?*

*Why didn't I get a bigger say in this decision?*

I paced back and forth, back and forth, even as my thoughts battled with each other ...

*Shit, what are we doing?*

*Life is a fleeting thing, and to just throw something like this away is retarded.*

*But they're not alive yet; they are only fetuses.*

*This will be something that will stay with us for the rest of our lives*

I panicked and started to rush toward the door to tell Louise not to do it so we could have more time to think about this.

But more minutes had passed than I'd thought. I had been caught up in my world for longer than I'd realized. As I approached the door, I stopped and dropped my cigarette as I saw Louise coming the other way, her arms crossed and her body language closed off. She walked through the door with Julie, glanced at me, then continued to walk past me as if I wasn't even there. The look of pity that I got from Julie was the only interaction I would get with the world outside of my mind until I returned to work after the weekend.

So, with that, I buried it deep down. I thought I was taking one for the team. I decided I would never bring it up again unless she did first. I actually wouldn't end up talking about it to anyone except for just one time ...

It was late and I had used the car to do some shopping, so I dropped Louise off at work. I was to meet her out the front, but when she was more than fifteen minutes late, I decided to go in and see how much longer she would be. I was greeted at the door by a young lady about the same age as me.

"Hello, how can I help you?" she asked.

"Hello. Yes, I'm Adam, Louise's boyfriend, here to pick her up."

The look on her face immediately soured. "Oh, okay," she said, looking at me with disgust.

She walked away into the restaurant, and as she did, she passed another girl and stopped her, then whispered something to her—what I only could have interpreted as telling her who I was. The other girl's eyes lit up and she turned and said, "Oh, congratulations on the twins!"

My heart stopped, deathly still.

The other girl looked at her, clearly shocked, and whispered loudly, "Nooo!" Then she whispered silently into her ear, and the other girl's face turned as sour as the first's did when she found out who I was.

"You're the asshole who made her have an abortion!" the second girl said.

I felt gobsmacked, lost for words, and I could feel my pupils dilate and my eyes widen.

"You're an ass," she continued. "Louise is a lovely girl and she definitely deserves more than a guy like you. I tell you, I would never even—"

"Who the fuck do you think you are?" I growled. "First of all, you know nothing about me. Second, you know nothing about the situation. And third, mind your own fuckin' business. Now fuck off back there and tell Louise I'm waiting for her in the car."

And with that, I stormed out to the car. When Louise arrived, I said nothing. She looked nervous, and she could see I was enraged, but I said nothing, She had tried to

241

make herself feel better about the situation by making herself out to be a victim in all of this—put the blame on me so she could feel better about it. Once again, I just took it.

Things after that were just way too stale and awkward in that place, in that village, at work for her, and in my head for me.

Louise had been wanting to visit home for a while now, and it seemed like the perfect time to do so.

Plus, we had been having some problems with the old couple we were renting from.

I wasn't 100 percent sure why, though. They thought we were using too much hot water. They thought we were parking the car to close to the gate. They didn't like that Louise would get home late from work, etc. Stupid little petty reasons that weren't major things to us or any reasonable person, but apparently were the end of the world to them.

We ended up moving in with Martin and his wife after I told him about the situation. It was another brilliant show of their hospitality and kindness toward us. But it was only a temporary fix to a bigger problem. Things just weren't the same. And in a village like this, somehow it wouldn't be long before everyone knew what had happened, considering Louise hadn't kept it to herself.

So we decided to go home to Australia for Christmas, which was only about four weeks away. We would spend a couple weeks there visiting my family and hers, never speaking of recent events to each other or our families.

It was nice to visit home for a few weeks, mainly because it was a novelty, I think. To see people I hadn't seen for a long time, to catch up with family in a more intimate way than a phone call ... It would be the first time I would see my father since he'd told me he was diagnosed with cancer—six months after my nana had died from it.

242

Although he insisted it was nothing and that it was a type of cancer that most people overcame, I knew it would be good to see him and just see for myself, especially after what happened with my nana. I hadn't been told how sick she really was, and I didn't even know she was in hospital when she had been for a month. I also hadn't been told that it was the second time she was in hospital, due to her slipping and falling a few months ago. I was told nothing until she passed away. No chance to get to know that link in our family history a little better, no chance to say "Good-bye" or "I love you" one more time.

It didn't take long, though, for the novelty to wear off. It only takes a couple of weeks before you realize that nothing really changes at home and you start remembering all the reasons you left. So I was soon eager to get back overseas.

Our time in Upper Wraxall had been nice while it lasted, as it gave us a little more independence—to have our own place and our own space and even a vehicle to get around in. Unfortunately, we weren't saving enough money. It was great to live in a small English town living the local life for a while, but if it wasn't going to be forever, then we had to save some money for the future. While in Australia, it dawned on us that the quickest way to save money was live-in bar work—even though we really didn't enjoy the "incestuous" lifestyle in which you work, eat, sleep, and shit with the same people 24/7. It always eventually hits overload and everything comes to a boiling point, So we decided to do the live-in bar thing again, but this time I would just take a barman position and nothing at management level—first, so I could enjoy it a little bit more; second, because there was no way Louise wanted to work under me; and third, because we didn't want to be there for anywhere near the time of commitment I would have had to make to get hired as a manager. The decision made, it was time to move on it.

# CHAPTER 24

## LET'S DO IT ALL AGAIN

Louise understandably wanted more time at home in Australia, so I ended up going back to the UK alone at the outset. I didn't know at the time, but she was actually thinking about just staying at home and not ever coming back. She had firmly made up her mind at one stage, and the only thing that ended up changing it was how she watched herself fall back into the same life she had left behind last time she was home. She realized that it was not what she wanted. It had nothing to do with her undying love for me!

I stayed with Roy and Julie for a few weeks until I found work for both Louise and me in a place called Barston, a small town in Warwickshire close to Solihull and Birmingham.

It would be the same as we had done before: live-in bar and restaurant work, and it would turn out to be a pretty good place to spend the next four months. It paid the most we had ever received, and this was mostly due to the success of the restaurant and the good tips we would receive each week.

When I first started at the Bolt Shovel, the manager was a guy named Jeff. He was a jolly little, fat, balding fellow and was probably the most successful manager I had worked for.

The assistant managers were Crystal and Mike, two South Africans who had been living in the UK for a couple of years. I would become good friends with Mike, and we would spend many a night drinking pints of Guinness after work and sharing stories of the world. We also regularly talked about the three big topics that always seem to come up in drunken conversations when the deep philosophical type of inebriation kicks in: science, politics, and religion. We would often be joined by the other barman there, named Anthony, who was also South African, but when he joined us, it tended to turn into more of a conversation about how good it would be if our girlfriends all started to make out and various things along those lines.

There was a fairly high turnover of staff at that time in the pub. The place went through a lot of changes. It all started when Jeff decided to resign so he could start up his own place, as he wasn't actually the owner, just the manager. The actual owner was a man named Kent, and he had an evil reputation. He was a small man of about five-six, in his fifties, but you would be forgiven for thinking he was in his late sixties because the years really hadn't been kind to him, mostly because he hadn't been kind to himself. Years of alcohol and tobacco abuse had taken their toll. About a year before, he'd had a tumor removed from his vocal chords, due to the cigarette smoke that had forever damaged them. So when he would talk, he would do so quietly in a low, growling voice, which he had to push out from the bottom of the lungs, dribbling saliva all over himself as he went. He was definitely the type of man you would take pity on at first appearances, but as soon as he opened his mouth or you heard a couple of stories about him, you would change your mind. Kent used to come in once or maybe twice a week and stand at the end of the bar, then proceed to order a half a wine glass full of vodka with one ice cube in it. I didn't know that this was his regular drink, so I used to ask him every time that he came in what he wanted, until about the fourth time. He leaned over the bar and stared at me, with his beady little eyes showing the utmost sincere hatred for me.

"Now look here, you little cunt," he said. "I'm the fucking owner of this place, so you better learn my fuckin' drink or fuck off. You're lucky I'm not twenty years younger or I would have kicked the shit out of a smart-ass little fucking fuck like you the second time you asked."

Charming fellow ... Luckily, besides that brief interaction with me, he had nothing to do with the actual running of the place anymore.

After Jeff left, instead of promoting Mike to general manager as ever one presumed would happen, they hired a lady named Christine. She was in her late thirties, was from France, and had short, spiked, dark red hair. She was a nice lady most of the time, about as much as a boss should be, but unfortunately it didn't take long for Kent to disagree with the way she wanted to run things, including being too friendly to the staff. She was only there for maybe two months. Then, after she'd left, Kent promoted another French guy that Christine had hired to be her assistant manager—as by this time, Mike had endured enough and left to go work with Jeff in his new place. The new guy's name was Lonnie, and we would instantly clash heads.

Louise had returned by now and worked with me at the Bolt Shovel. We hadn't really talked about the abortion since it had happened. I guess we didn't really feel like it was something that needed to be discussed. Unfortunately, I think it planted a seed in both of us that wasn't going to be eliminated so easily. I think it was more on her side, and deep down, I think she never stopped blaming me for what had happened. It started to divide us again. Although it wasn't really brought up, I think it was the reason why a lot of other things seemed to be going wrong between us. She would be angry if I wanted to stay up drinking with Mike. I would get angry if she wanted to do something different than me on our day off. A whole lot of little things that just continued to build frustration in our relationship. It eventually became too much and she moved out into another live-in position, but we still stayed in a relationship.

The place she now worked was only about ten

246

minutes away, so we still managed to see a lot of each other, especially with me having use of the company car.

That company car actually was also how I learnt to drive a manual. I had tried a couple of times on my sister's car at home when I was younger, but never could get hold of it enough to get the hang of it. So, on my days off, I would ask a coworker friend of mine, nicknamed Lithy (he was from Lithuania), to drive it out of the car park, then down the road so I could practice in it away from the pub—so no one would hear me grinding the gears, as you inevitably do when you learn. It didn't take long to get the hang of it, so I soon could drive it in and out of the car park myself. Then, by just running around in it, I taught myself how to drive a manual.

Another moment from my time at the Bolt Shovel that really sticks in my mind was when I was sitting on my bed one day, just flicking through a magazine, and I came across one of the most awesome pictures I had seen for a long time. When I travel, I quite often have different reasons for visiting different places. I like going to a country I know nothing about and then exploring, or going to a place where I know a person to visit and check it out, but my favorite is to have a specific mission to be a highlight for my trip. Like the Taj Mahal in India, the pyramids of Giza in Egypt, or Mount Everest in Nepal. For me, flicking through this magazine and seeing a picture of this place, it would instantly become an inspiration and a place I would have to visit.

It was a picture of an old wall with a massive tree growing out of it. Maybe three hundred years ago, a tree had dropped a seed on top of the wall and it started to grow. As it got bigger, its need for water and nutrients increased, so it started spreading its roots toward the ground the quickest way possible: right off of the side of the wall. It looked incredible. It was like this place had just one day been deserted and over the years Mother Nature had slowly

247

started to reclaim the land that had been once stolen from her. That wall was a part of the largest religious complex in the world, with an age of eight hundred years old. It was Angkor Wat in Cambodia, and it was now implanted in my memory and became a desired destination to explore. I would end up seeing it for myself less than a year later, but that's another story.

I guess in hindsight, I could say that while I was working at the Bolt Shovel, I acted like a bit of an asshole on occasions toward Lonnie. He had even tried to help me somewhat. One time after having an argument with Louise in the work van, I punched the windshield in frustration, not too hard, but I did end up breaking it. So I went up to Lonnie and told him the truth. To which, he laughed and replied, "Shit, no way, Adam! That must have been one hell of a punch. Don't worry, I will take care of it." And with that, no one else ever found out the truth of what had happened to the windshield, because Lonnie had made up a cover story for me. Still, on the flip side, a few weeks later he stopped the use of the company car, saying that, "Nowhere else would you get the use of a car, so why should we let you have this privilege when it is costing us money?"

Lonnie tried to give me leeway, but I didn't like the way things were changing, so I was a stubborn ass. Plus, we just had personality types that clashed, no matter how we tried to be gentlemen toward each other. He gave me plenty of time to change and conform to the new way things were to be done under his rule, but nobody liked the way he ran things, not even the customers. Unfortunately, I was the one stubborn enough to stand up and say something, albeit unintentionally.

I guess our differences of opinion also had a lot to do with the fact that I was overqualified to be a barman. I had, after all, been the general manager of a pub, although I never told anyone about that at the Bolt Shovel, so my

248

opinions there weren't always appreciated. I guess I could have come across as some smart-ass who thought he knew everything, so I did try to keep my opinions mostly to myself and only give them when they were asked for.

But all the bickering between Lonnie and me came to a head one day. Most of the staff had turned over in the past few months, mainly because of the way Lonnie ran things. He even cut the salary of the pot washer, a guy we called "Potty," because Lonnie thought he was overpaid. Potty had been washing dishes there for about five years, and for his loyalty and work ethic, which involved some long hours, he had gotten consistent pay raises. He wasn't earning a fortune, but he was earning as much as a junior chef. His wages were good enough that he was halfway through paying off a mortgage at the time and he was only twenty-one. A fair choice, I guess, if you wanted to spend ten years paying off a house by washing dishes, while renting out the place and still living at home with your mum. (This situation came across all the more stranger because he was probably the most intelligent person in that place.)

So Lonnie came into the bar and approached the four staff who were standing at the bar having a little conversation during a non-busy time. Everything that needed to be done had been, but that didn't stop Lonnie from saying in his most arrogant French accent, "Right, what are you all doing standing here? There is always something to do. Let's take a vote. Who thinks that it is the right thing for you all to be standing here doing nothing?"

No one wanted to try and explain it to him, so we all said nothing.

"Right, then do something."

And with that, he strutted toward the door to the back garden, so I turned around and said, "Right, let's have a vote. Who thinks Lonnie should go and fuck himself?"

I laughed and raised my hand, as did the others—

until they all turned and walked away suddenly. I stopped and turned around to see Lonnie standing by the door.

"Adam, we need to talk," was his response. So we went into the restaurant and sat down.

"Adam," he said, "I am letting you go. You are the best barman I have ever seen, but we don't get along."

I had been fired.

Not exactly a surprise, and I wasn't too broken up about it, really. Luckily, Lonnie did give me two weeks' notice, time enough to find a job and a new place to live.

Lonnie only stayed at the Bolt Shovel for maybe six more months before he himself was fired.

So we were to try it all again. Louise also quit her job, and we were off to work in a new place called the Bel and Dragon. This would be the last live-in bar position I would ever have.

We would work at the Bel for about ten weeks, just long enough to top up with a bit more money and then we were off. Off to explore the world for an undetermined amount of time, a journey that would keep us on the road for about a year by the end of it.

So we were off. We were free. This had been our goal for a long time. We had the wind at our backs, cash in our pockets, open minds, and our hearts to guide us to wherever we would end up.

This was the beginning of yet another chapter of life for us …

43878658R00154

Made in the USA
Lexington, KY
15 August 2015